I WILL WITNESS

YOUR PATH TO SHARING JESUS CHRIST

WITHOUT FEAR

WADE WHITE

This book was published so that others may know Christ. Please visit our website and tell your story about witnessing:

www.iwillwitness.com

TABLE OF CONTENTS

WHY I WROTE THIS BOOK

I wrote this book after years of serving as a youth minister and finding the same problem – Christians are afraid to share their faith. The fear of witnessing was nearly universal for every student I taught. And its not only a problem for youth but also for those who have been a Christian for years.

Most Christians say – "I will invite friends to church, I will sing Christian songs and I will wear Christian t-shirts, but I'm afraid to witness." We have allowed the lies of Satan and our fear of witnessing to silence us for far too long.

So I set out to write a very detailed but easy to read book so others may overcome their fear to witness. This book is enjoyable to read while life changing. Although it is written with new Christians in mind it's clear nearly every Christian struggles to witness. Just because you have been a Christian since you were young doesn't mean you easily share Christ, if not, this book is for you.

I believe one of the most important things we could ever learn or teach someone else is how to be a bold witness for the Saving Grace of Jesus Christ. When you finish this book I believe you will answer the call of Jesus to share the good news of His Salvation by saying YES! Lord, I WILL WITNESS!

This Book is dedicated to my first students I taught to witness without fear: Barrett Blackburn, Billy Dorroh, Sam Gray, Lillian Kessel, Bryant Millikan, Shelby Murphy, Jacob Snyder, Brandon White and Jenna White.

WHY YOU SHOULD READ THIS BOOK

Have you ever been on vacation and decided to take a walk on a nature trail? If so, why did you choose to get out of your air conditioned car and walk this trail? Was it because you believed there was something more spectacular to see?

We like to believe the trail always ends at the most scenic point. It usually happens that way. I have never found a nature trail that started at an amazing waterfall and ended in a parking lot. It is quite the opposite. The trail exists as proof something even better awaits at the end of the path.

When I walk back to my car after finishing a trail hike, I'm often asked by people just starting out, "is it worth the walk?" When I answer, "I wouldn't walk it again to see that," the person stops walking, shoves the kids back in the car and drives somewhere new. However, if I say, "it's the coolest waterfall I have seen," they continue up the trail without hesitation.

Likewise let me encourage you to take this path to a life changing journey. In this book, you will learn how to witness. You will learn salvation from start to finish and how to overcome your fear of witnessing. You will learn how to pray for the lost and how to share Christ when the opportunity arises. My purpose in this book is to give you knowledge so you will become bold enough to witness.

Learning to tell others about Jesus will be life changing for you and packed with eternal rewards and earthly blessings. As we learn to lead others to Jesus we also discover our place and purpose in this world. We begin to see through God's eyes and it changes our perspective on life. So walk with me in learning how to see things through God's eyes and how to become His witness.

This book is for ordinary Christians. Churchy words are banned in this book so a theological degrees are not needed.

Is it worth the walk? Yes! It is.

Following Jesus down this path is an exciting adventure you will never regret. Today, your journey can begin. There IS something more spectacular at the end of this path. Turning back is simply not an option. Be bold and find out what lies at the end of this path. For you will never know the destination of a path you refuse to take.

CHAPTER 1. HERO

It is midnight as I finish writing. I shut down my computer and the monitor clicks off. I notice the darkness. It closes around me like falling rain. My eyes adjust. Borrowing from the moon I can find enough light to find my way in the dark.

This darkness around me is not the same as I experienced in a cave I recently toured. Once inside the cave I shut off my flashlight and there it was - pure darkness - unlike I have ever experienced. My hand, even at the tip of my nose, couldn't be seen. Nowhere else have I found such darkness. True darkness requires the absolute, complete elimination of light.

That must have been what she saw, true darkness. Her wide-opened eyes searched for any glimpse of light, but saw none. She couldn't move up or down, left or right. Her feet dangled in thin air over a dark pit. She was squeezed from both sides and totally helpless to save herself. Her gasps for help unheard. The only sound was the pounding of her little heart.

This 18-month-old little girl had fallen into a Midland, Texas well trapped 22 feet below the surface of the Earth. Her life literally hung in the balance. The whole world was gripped by the news of the child trapped in the well. Little "Baby Jessica," McClure was on everyone's mind.

The rescue workers of Midland scrambled to get "baby Jessica" out of the well as news cameras kept the whole world informed. Midland's finest dug a hole through pure rock adjacent to Jessica's well in order to dislodge her. These heroes never gave up on baby Jessica until she was safely snatched from the jaws of death.

Below is an excerpt from msnbc.com, from an interview by Matt Lauer in 2007, with a grown up "Baby Jessica."

"Jessica was wedged in the pipe 22 feet down. Rescuers piped fresh air and heat down to her while they labored nonstop on the rescue shafts. When she was finally pulled out, a filthy but alert 18-month-old girl wrapped in gauze and strapped to a backboard, rescuers cheered and church bells rang out. There was even a White House reception with President George H. W. Bush and First Lady Barbara Bush. She had become "Everybody's Baby," the title of an ABC TV movie about her rescue." (Source: MSNBC.COM transcript)

People everywhere prayed for "Baby Jessica." Glued to television sets America watched and hoped for the safe recovery of this little girl. When she was pulled alive from this dark pit - the celebration began. Church bells rang out all across America. The world honored the heroes who let nothing stand in the way of rescue. They were completely committed to guarding the life of "Baby Jessica."

HERO TO THE WORLD

I need to ask you a very important question. Ever imagine yourself as a hero? If you had to decide which character you would be in this story, would you want to be the one caught in the well, or the one who saved her? I would want to be the hero, wouldn't you? We all want to be the hero in the story. Talk about instant fame! Try being the one who saved "Baby

7

Jessica!" Imagine the whole world watching and cheering as you save the life of this little helpless girl.

Many of us live with the hope that just one day we will be the hero. We hope to do something that will make people stand to their feet and cheer. We want to matter to someone, somehow, somewhere, some day.

This heroic drive is deep in our hearts. That is why we cheer heroes. But there is one big problem. Being a "hero to the world" may not be as great as it seems. Most of us want to be the world's hero just once. But be careful, you may want to be a hero for the wrong reasons.

"What's wrong with being a hero?" Absolutely nothing. The danger is in whose hero you seek to become. Take for instance, Robert O'Donnell. Do you recognize that name?

Staten Island (NY) Advance staff writer David Andreatta, in an article entitled "Coming Down From the Hero High," wrote these words about Robert O'Donnell in 2002:

"If you don't recognize Robert O'Donnell's name, chances are you remember what he did. O'Donnell was the paramedic who slithered down a tomblike tunnel to free 18-month-old Jessica McClure from a deserted well in Midland, Texas, in 1987. He ascended overnight to the rank of American hero, with a parade, a White House salute and countless TV appearances.

But gradually the news media's restless eye shifted away. A book deal failed to materialize. A cameo movie appearance was left on the cutting room floor. Eventually, O'Donnell's marriage crumbled, and an addiction to prescription drugs cost him his job with the Midland Fire Department.

On April 19, 1995, he went over the edge as he watched firefighters on television racing the clock in Oklahoma City. "When those rescuers are through, they're going to need lots of help," he reportedly told his mother. "I don't mean for a couple of days or weeks, but for years."

Four days after the bombing, Robert put a shotgun to his head and pulled the trigger."

Hero to the world. The instant fame and roller-coaster ride from being anonymous to famous to anonymous again hit Robert hard. What happened to this hero? Why would he shoot himself? I can't say for sure because I did not know him, but I do understand how this world works. Here is my opinion. Could being a hero to the world have destroyed him?

Maybe Robert allowed his worth to be built upon what the world thought of him. Maybe when the media were done with Robert they just threw him away, moved on and maybe it broke him. When we become more interested in whether we are pleasing our friends instead of pleasing God it becomes exhausting.

What does Jesus say about building on things other than Him?

"Therefore, everyone who hears these words of Mine and acts on them will be like a sensible man who built his house on the rock. The rain fell, the rivers rose, and the winds blew and pounded that house. Yet it didn't collapse, because its

9

foundation was on the rock. But everyone who hears these words of Mine and doesn't act on them will be like a foolish man who built his house on the sand. The rain fell, the rivers rose, the winds blew and pounded that house, and it collapsed. And its collapse was great!" (Matt. 7:24-27 HCSB)

It goes to show just how relevant the Word of God is to us today. Look at what He says, "The rain fell, the rivers rose, the winds blew and pounded that house, and it collapsed. And its collapse was great!" If you are building your life upon what others think of you, guess what? Your collapse will be great!

The majority of people who find their approval from the world are eventually destroyed by it. Robert may have been standing on shifting sands. His worth may have been tied to the fame. When it crumbled so did his spirit. Do you tie your worth to what your friends at school or work think of you?

We seek to fit in with the "in" crowd. We want the right clothes, cell phone or nice car. One day everyone loves you and the next day your own best friend betrays you. How do you react to that? How you react may be tied to who's hero you want to become.

Whether your friends think you are the best is simply the wrong source to determine your worth. Kids at school may vote you "class hero" today and "class clown" tomorrow. If you are sick of constantly not measuring up to those standards I have a treat for you. You can actually be a true hero simply by seeing yourself through God's eyes.

What if, starting today, you decide to no longer let your friends decide if you are a hero? What if, starting today, you see through the eyes of God and let Him decide if you are a hero?

SEEING THROUGH GOD'S EYES

Suppose you have just saved "Baby Jessica," and the world is knocking your door down to give you all it has to offer. Do you accept or run for the hills? Well, I would take them up on it. I see nothing wrong with the applause and interest the world would give. I think that is a natural reaction to a hero, and Robert is a hero.

The problem is when the applause becomes our measurement of success. It's almost as if we adopt an applause meter for our life. The more applause we get the better. We start to believe the higher the applause level the greater our success. However, as the applause decreases, so will our self-worth. We may allow the world's attention to become a drug we need to feel good. We do whatever we need to do, even if it's wrong, to keep the applause meter high.

Once we are considered cool by the 'in crowd' we may do anything not to mess that up. We will give up telling others about Jesus or inviting them to church because we fear they will laugh at us for being a Jesus Freak.

Now, suppose you were the hero and God gave your self-worth to you. If your goal is to glorify God, how would this situation be different? When the TV cameras show up, you will be excited, but as the weeks of accolades end, you will feel the same about yourself. You will not go into depression mode because the parade ended.

Why? Because the world did not create you. Who you are today was not granted by the news media. Your name is still known by the only One who matters, Jesus Christ. You know your value was determined two thousand years ago upon Calvary Hill. Your worth was paid in full upon a cross with the priceless blood of Jesus.

When the promise keeper Himself guarantees your worth, you never lose your value. See how different things are when our hero status comes from God instead of the world?

When we see the world through God's eyes, we see things differently. Our lives will take on new meaning and purpose. As we gaze through God's eyes, we will see nothing is small and unnoticed; everything we do matters. Even the smallest things we do for God, though unnoticed by the world, will one day be a reward in Heaven. This reward will never pass away. Understanding the importance of the small things we do will get us on our way to becoming a hero to One.

REWARDS FROM GOD OR PEOPLE

It is very important to understand that everything we do has eternal consequences. Many of us go through life believing we are small and do not impact anyone else's life. Oh, how wrong you are if that is your mindset. Everything you do is known by God and almost everything you do affects others around you in ways you may never know until you stand in Heaven.

Here is a real life example:

Brandy, a youth member at my church, was in school one day and felt she should give a small pocket testament Bible to a girl in the hallway. Classes had just started; already running late, Brandy told the girl she wanted her to have this little Bible. Brandy walked away and nothing seemed to happen.

A few weeks later Brandy, received a phone call from this girl. She stated, "I read the pocket testament, started going to church and tonight my friends led me to Christ!" You see, the simple act of giving this girl a pocket testament set things in motion for her salvation. She was so thankful that she even wrote a song for Brandy describing the event. Such a simple little thing became a very big deal to someone who was trapped in a dark hole and needed a hero.

Brandy did not realize she was being a hero. She simply acted in a way she felt would glorify God. The salvation was an awesome thing, but not the reason why a reward in Heaven awaits Brandy. Her reward is tied to the simple act of giving away the pocket testament. This reward may not be in her hands today, but will be an eternal reward that will never pass away. Let's see this through God's eyes, to capture the significance of this little event.

WHAT DID THE WORLD SEE?

Brandy handed the pocket testament to this lost girl and quietly walked away? No one knew what Brandy had done. There were no pats on the back and offers of interviews to describe the moment. Brandy heard no cheering crowds. No White House meeting with the President and First Lady, nor parades through the downtown square. Brandy quietly went

13

on about her day as if nothing ever happened – and to the world nothing did.

WHAT DID GOD SEE?

God was separating this girl from her captor, Satan, so she could clearly hear and respond to the Gospel. God set up this Divine Appointment so that these two girls would cross paths in the hallway at the right moment. God was working all around this one moment for Brandy to witness. And this is what this book is all about, knowing how God is working around you in the salvation process.

Brandy, as God sees her, became a hero to One. Though nothing but silence was heard here on earth, all of Heaven shook as the Saints in the presence of the Angels danced around the throne of God for the salvation of this one soul.

One day in Heaven these two will meet again. Brandy will be rewarded for her small act. Her reward will far outweigh anything this world could ever offer and it will never fade away. Nothing the world can do will ever take away the reward in Heaven that awaits the heroes involved in this one salvation. Such a tiny little thing, yet such great rewards.

Billy, a fourth grader, invited his friend Josh to church. Josh came but didn't like going to church that much so he never came back. What was Billy to do? He asked Josh to come back to church but he refused. Billy took the next step. Since Josh wouldn't come to church to learn about Jesus, Billy would take Jesus to Josh at school.

Billy began his quest to see his friend come to know Jesus by praying for Josh. Then Billy gave Josh a pocket testament at school and continued to pray for him. After a few weeks of praying, Josh wanted to know more about Jesus. That is when Josh, Billy and Jenna sat down during their break to talk about Jesus and how He saves. Josh eventually accepted Jesus as his Savior.

Who are the heroes? Billy and Jenna are heroes for taking Jesus to their school and being His witnesses. There are now rewards waiting in Heaven for both. Billy and Jenna decided it was more important to them to see their friend know Jesus than to play at recess. Because they decided to be a hero to their friend, they both will receive special rewards one day in Heaven. But not because of the salvation – but because they witnessed.

Billy and Jenna both play basketball on Saturday mornings. They both get applause from the fans when they make a great play. But when they witness there are no cheers to push them on. They do it to Glorify God. Though few others see what they have done, God sees and will remember.

Which reward appeals to you most? The rewards given by the world that will vanish in time or rewards from God that last forever? How you answer that question will determine how you spend your life.

As always, nothing describes it better than scripture:

"Do not love this world nor the things it offers you, for when you love the world, you do not have the love of the Father in you. For the world offers only a craving for physical pleasure, a craving for everything we see, and pride in our achievements and possessions. These are not from the Father, but are from this world. And this world is fading away, along with everything that people crave. But anyone who does what pleases God will live forever." (I John 2:15-17 NLT)

Everything else passes away. The only things truly real and lasting are those done for God. It comes down to what lies in your heart. Is the love of God enough in your life to do small things for God? If you act to glorify God, you are storing up treasures in Heaven that you will enjoy for eternity.

"Don't store up treasures here on earth, where moths eat them and rust destroys them, and where thieves break in and steal. Store your treasures in Heaven, where moths and rust cannot destroy, and thieves do not break in and steal. Wherever your treasure is, there the desires of your heart will also be." (Matthew 6:19-21 NLT)

To store up treasures in Heaven, you must change your perspective on life. You must change whom you seek to please. I believe the benefit of this book in your life will hinge on whether or not you will be seeking the applause of your friends or the applause of God.

PLAYING FOR THE HOME TEAM?

If the rewards in Heaven are so amazing, then why do we not do more to earn them? The problem is we may be playing for the HOME TEAM.

Have you ever watched a sports event on TV where the away team beats the home team? If the game is played far from the away team's hometown their fans probably will not be in the stands. You may notice the awkward quiet that falls over the crowd when the away team wins.

Sometimes the away team will make a spectacular play, yet it seems as if no one cares. No applause, no cheers, no banners. The silence is almost deafening. I notice this when listening to my favorite baseball team on the radio. If we are playing away and there is a base hit, I know immediately my team got the hit. The crowd is quiet. This really makes it tough on the away team to keep momentum when the crowd doesn't react to their play.

Why does the home team always seem to have the advantage? I think the biggest advantage is the friendly crowd. You have seen and possibly played a game for the home team.

A good play is immediately applauded and cheered. This is home team advantage. Typically, the crowd is a major factor in the attitude and performance of their team. On most days, the picture is clear: the more enthusiastic the crowd, the better the team's performance.

It doesn't take a fifth grader to know a cheering crowd can pump up a team and completely turn a game around. I attended a football game of my alma mater, the University of Kentucky. UK was on a winning streak and this game against Mississippi State should have been ours. However, our crowd was quiet. So was the team. The crowd was waiting for something to cheer about; the team was waiting for the crowd. This led to a stalemate between the fans and the players that contributed to a loss for the home team.

The lack of excitement from the crowd sometimes causes the team to lose its spark. It is difficult to make a great play but hear nothing from the crowd except the guy selling peanuts in the upper deck.

The team that plays dead because the crowd is dead simply needs to hear the applause. They need the benefit of instant applause for their work. They thrive off the sound of the crowd cheering the team name. This is playing for the **home team.**

Playing for the home team is how many Christians live their lives. They will donate a large sum of money only when others will know about it. They will help at church only when they will get credit or a pat on the back. Playing for the home team causes someone to do good things only when others are looking. They need the satisfaction of instant praise from others.

You may be playing for the home team. Do you act like a good church kid only when your parents or adults are looking? Do you do nice things only when you will get rewarded for it?

PLAYING FOR THE AWAY TEAM

Playing for the away team does not require a friendly crowd's approval to achieve success. Why? Because the players know that, somewhere in the distance, their fans stand in living rooms cheering and applauding. When they finally get back home, the thing they achieved will be remembered, talked about and rewarded.

But at this moment, although their reward is delayed, they continue to play hard. When they score or make a great play they do not hear applause because the cheers for what they do will come one day when they are back home. Their reward is delayed, but guaranteed.

Here are Jesus' own words speaking about playing for the home and away team.

"Watch out! Don't do your good deeds publicly, to be admired by others, for you will lose the reward from your Father in Heaven. When you give to someone in need, don't do as the hypocrites do – blowing trumpets in the synagogues and streets to call attention to their acts of charity! I tell you the truth, they have received all the reward they will ever get. But when you give to someone in need, don't let your left hand know what your right hand is doing. Give your gifts in private, and your Father, who sees everything, will reward you." (Matthew 6: 1-4 NLT)

Jesus makes it very clear that if we are working for Him, we cannot always expect applause from our friends. Sometimes we may even be disliked because we listen to Christian music more than other music. We may get left out because we don't like to watch "R" rated movies or curse in every joke.

Jesus is clearly stating playing for the home team will not be rewarded in Heaven. If we are doing things simply to get the praise of our friends and church family our only reward will be the applause they give us, nothing more.

When we are on God's team we are on the away team. Our rewards and cheers are far away and delayed. One day, when we are home in Heaven, Jesus will grant us rewards for the things done in His Name. It's then that we will hear the cheers and excitement for our work done in the home team's stadium. We will be part of the victory parade in Heaven and hear the words, "welcome home, you good and faithful servant, job well done."

Brandy played for the away team when she handed off that pocket testament. Billy and Jenna spent their recess playing for the away team. They didn't hear the cheers. The world fell silent around them. Fortunately, they were not looking for the applause of the world. They were looking for the approval of Jesus.

Leading others to Jesus mostly goes unnoticed by a world consumed by the spotlight of recognition. You are now invited to join the few who play for the away team. It is an uphill battle and the applause may rarely come. But playing for the away team also means you are playing for an audience of One, God.

Before we go on this journey, we must take the first step of answering this question: Who is Jesus to you?

Chapter 2. Lost

Where Am I?

One cold, rainy day I took my youth group on an adventure in the woods. We began our journey in a wooded area that was familiar to me, but not the students. Throughout the day, as we proceeded toward the final destination, I would teach a new lesson at each stop. During one of the lessons, I broke the boys and girls apart and gave minimal directions on how to find the next meeting place. My assistant youth minister, Brian Snyder, planned to keep an eye on the girls from a distance as they moved to their next meeting place.

The girls were taken to the headwater of a small stream that deepened as it traveled along. I started them at this spot and handed them a piece of paper that read: "Follow as the water flows." I then walked away without a word.

Brian went up on the hill to watch for the girls as they made their way to the next meeting place. They never made it. This area had hills on all three sides. The water could only flow one way but they never made it to the next destination. Brian and I went back to the spot looking for clues. They seemed to have vanished. I simply could not figure out why they would walk up a hill if the clue was to "go as the water flows." I searched the hills, and walked back and forth through the woods. I couldn't believe they were lost!

After an hour of searching I finally found them sitting on a log a few hundred feet from where we first started our journey.

I was so relieved and glad to see them. They were glad to see me too, but they were not as relieved as I.

They had walked in circles trying to figure out the deep meaning inside my note and had gone the wrong way. But they never felt as if they were lost. They just decided to sit down and wait for me to show up.

I, on the other hand, considered them to be very lost, because I knew where they should be and they were not. I searched for them everywhere while they talked, laughed, walked in circles and picked up rocks as souvenirs. They didn't realize just how lost they really were.

This story serves as an example of how a lot of your friends, and possibly you, are walking around in the world today. Is there any chance you could be wandering around lost like these girls and not even know it? They really didn't know their next destination nor how to get there. They just wandered around hoping for the best.

Until they were convinced they were lost, they couldn't be saved. I wasn't a hero to them until they realized they had been lost the whole time.

What about you?

Can you point to a time when you were lost and then found? If not, could you still be lost?

This section will be good for you on two levels. 1) You can use it to make sure you know you are saved, 2) you can use it as knowledge to lead others to Jesus in the future.

LOST AND FOUND

Prior to one of my first classes I taught about witnessing called, Camp Witness, I showed Billy a special tree in the park where we met. I called it tree 3. I asked Billy not to tell anyone else about this special tree.

During class I asked who could find tree 3. None of them could point it out. Why? None of them had ever been to tree 3. Only Billy could take us to this special tree because he had been there before.

If you want to take people to the foot of the Cross to meet Jesus, then you better know how to get there. If you want others to know Jesus then you better know Him too. You can't take someone where you have not been yourself. Otherwise, you will simply wander around with those to whom you're trying to bring to Christ. So before we move into the heart of witnessing, we must be sure of the most important question: Who is Jesus Christ to you?

Jesus said,

"Not everyone who says to me, 'Lord, Lord!' Will enter the kingdom of Heaven, but only the one who does the will of my father in Heaven. On that day many will say to Me, 'Lord, Lord didn't we prophesy in Your name, drive out demons in Your name, and do many miracles in Your Name?' Then I will announce to them 'I never knew you! Depart from Me you lawbreakers!'" (Matt. 7: 21-23 HCSB)

This scripture really should make us think. There are many in America who claim to be Christian who may be very surprised on judgment day. Many who stand before Jesus will not enter Heaven even though they may think they have a free ticket to ride. They will be shocked and horrified when Jesus says, "Depart from Me for I never knew you."

What!? Jesus doesn't know someone? No, no, no that's not the meaning here. It means He never had a personal relationship with you. Not because He was not capable of knowing you, but because you chose not to really know Him. You never invited Jesus to be your savior and meant it.

"Hey, I believe Jesus is real," you might say. Oh yeah? So does Satan, but he isn't getting in. So yes, my friend, this is a very important subject and you must get it right. If not, everything you will ever do "for the Lord" will count for nothing on Judgment Day. You must first know Jesus as your Savior.

Becoming a born again Christian is the most important thing you will ever do in your life because it will determine where you live forever and ever. That place will either be in Heaven, with Jesus, or in Hell, totally separated from Him. Wouldn't it be smart to make sure you got this right? Please read on.

THE FIRST QUESTION IS THE MOST IMPORTANT

Imagine yourself in a large auditorium sitting at a little wooden desk. As you look around, you see her far away - the school teacher sitting behind her large desk. She stands and slowly walks over to you. A ream of paper tucked under one arm and a finger to her chin. On your desk she drops a huge stack of paper and a pencil. Looking down her nose at you she says, "Here is your test."

You glance down and begin flipping through pages and pages of test questions. Sweat beads form along your brow. You look back up to catch her stare as she says in a low voice. "If you want to know, there are 147,456 questions on your test. Good luck." You sit in amazement. Then she says, "Oh, and one other thing, if you miss the first question and get the next 147,455 questions correct, you still flunk. You may begin."

You cry out, "That's impossible. How can I only miss one question and still fail? That's not fair!"

She says, "You can miss many questions – it's the first question that will cause you to flunk. Good Luck!"

The large clock on the wall ticks off seconds as you decide what to do next. Running out of options, you start the test.

With pencil in hand you read the first question:

Question #1: Who is Jesus Christ to you?

There is no skipping this question. You must answer it. How you answer this question will determine everything. A perfect score on the rest of the test won't matter if you miss this one. This is where your time must be spent.

Many people try to skip this question until they are older. Many people will try to answer every life question while leaving this most important question for later. But here is the problem with that strategy.

YOUR TEST MAY END AT ANY MOMENT

When you understand none of us are promised a long life all those times you spent daydreaming in Church or Sunday School flood back into your mind. You wish you'd listened. There is no more guessing, no more pretending. The maker of the test and the One who will eventually grade the test already knows your answer.

The question is do you?

I have a pleasant surprise for you. The test maker has already taken care of everything and made this an open book test. That's right! You can use the Bible! He also will allow you to have your very own personal tutor. You can even use the next few pages of this book as a guide to determine your answer to this question. The answer is not hidden. Jesus died to provide you the answer to this question. Please do not die without knowing it, without knowing Him. **Your clock is ticking.**

DID YOU MEET BRO. EAGER PANTS?

The first part of knowing who Jesus is to you comes with the understanding that YOU must make this choice to be saved. YOU must make the commitment. No one else can do this for you. You can pretend to have the answer correct, but God is not fooled. There are people walking around right now with a false sense of salvation thinking they are saved simply because someone told them so.

I have counseled many who came forward at a church service in years past wanting to be saved but instead were given a false sense of salvation. There are many who responded during a church service or religious event and as they came forward wanting their questions answered, there at the end of the aisle stood the person I call - Bro. Eager Pants.

Bro. Eager Pants simply answered question #1 for the lost person instead of leading them to Jesus.

The conversation may have gone something like this, "so, you want to get saved young lady?" You say "uh huh." Bro. Eager Pants then prays over you and announces to the church you are saved and going to Heaven.

Not necessarily! Unless YOU commit to Jesus you are still as lost as when you burst out of the pew. It is not the prayer he prays for you; it is the commitment to Jesus Christ you make that counts.

My sister-in-law experienced this as a youth. She met Sister Eager Pants who proclaimed her saved when she was young. Then she wrestled with her false sense of salvation through the rest of her teenage years. She had never been saved. It wasn't until she was 19 years old that she admitted she was still lost.

She knew all the right answers but lacked making Jesus her Lord and Savior. Sister Eager Pants took that chance away from her. She was prayed over, pronounced "saved," but it wasn't real.

KNOWING I'M SAVED

Imagine you are standing on the ocean shore as waves lap against your ankles. Your eyes scan the horizon. See that beautiful sailboat passing by with one man and two young boys aboard? Keep an eye on that vessel, because something is about to happen that may affect you for a lifetime.

This story, changed slightly, is from a story that appeared on the Internet in 2000, I believe its source was a book of inspirational tales published that year, *Stories for a Faithful Heart*. (Titled "The Father's Anguishing Decision"), attributing it to Carla Muir. I give her credit for this story.

You may one day retell this story to lead someone to Christ. I have used it and it's a great story to explain the love of God.

The two boys had been looking forward to this sailing trip all summer long. This day finally came for these boys as Captain Dad barked out orders to his small but lively crew.

After hours of sailing the boys find a few minutes to relax. They kick back and enjoy the spoils of their hard work as first time sailors. What a day it's been on the open seas. The boys welcome the cool breeze as they splash in the salty water.

While they are relaxing I want to introduce you to these boys. Jacob is Captain Dad's only son. Jacob accepted Jesus as his Lord and Savior about one year ago. Jacob and his friend, Brandon, have been best buds for about five years. Brandon's parents do not attend church, so hearing about Jesus is new to him. But that hasn't stopped Jacob. Jacob continues to witness to his best friend whenever the opportunity presents itself. These two twelve year old boys had been planning and working Captain Dad for weeks so they could go out sailing. Today was a dream come true.

A gust of cool wind spins their small vessel signaling a change in weather. Captain Dad looks up to see dark clouds forming on the horizon. Without drawing much concern from the boys, he orders them back to work so they can make landfall before dark. But the gathering clouds approach quickly. The storm makes its presence known by thundering warnings to those who dare play in its path. It is now a race to the shore.

The storm, much faster than their small boat, tosses waves over the deck of the boat. Dad quickly orders the sails to be dropped to avoid being toppled by the high winds. Making it to land is no longer an option; staying alive becomes their only battle.

Wave after wave tests their strength to hold on. Will the next be their last? Suddenly, a large wave hits the boat, nearly capsizing it. Jacob and Brandon are thrown into the dark water.

The Father watches in horror as Jacob is pulled in one direction and Brandon in another. Their screams for help muffled by the crashing waves. He grabs the life buoy to save the boys, but as he begins to throw it into the ocean he realizes he has only one aboard. He had prepared for fun, not tragedy.

As the boys float farther away, he cries out, "God please help me!" The ocean will devour both boys unless he acts quickly. He knows he can only save one. "Save the lost friend," his soul cries out, but his heart moans, "Save my son."

The Father knew when his son passed from this life, he would enter into an amazing paradise with Jesus Christ. But

Brandon was lost; he would go to Hell forever separated from Jacob and God. They would never see each other again.

With tears in his eyes the Father yells, "I love you son." And throws the life buoy to Brandon. The Father watches his only son's hand sink slowly into the dark waves. Brandon is saved, but Jacob is gone.

As a father this story always tears at my heart. What a hard choice that would be to watch your son disappear into the water while saving another boy. This story is a good comparison of our relationship with God.

You and I are just like Brandon floating away from God's boat. Without the sacrifice of God's only Son, Jesus, we too will die. I am thankful Jesus paid the price for you and me so I may have eternal life back in God's Boat.

As Brandon was drowning, no one else could grab that life buoy for him. It had to be thrown within his reach, but grabbing this life buoy was completely up to him. Have you grabbed the life buoy - Jesus Christ? Do you fully understand accepting Jesus is your ONLY WAY too?

Jesus said,

"I am the way, the truth, and the life. No one comes to the Father except through Me."(John 14:6 HCSB)

REALIZE YOU ARE LOST

Your first step is to realize you are a sinner.

"For all have sinned and fall short of the Glory of God." (Romans 3:23 HCSB).

When you are a sinner, you are no longer in God's boat. You are treading water in sin-filled darkness. Only one man lived a life free of sin, and that was Jesus. Guess what? You are not Him. Neither am I. This is usually the easiest part about coming to Christ; most of us understand we have done wrong things in our life. If you have ever told one lie or disobeyed your parents just once, you have sinned.

YOU CAN'T SAVE YOURSELF

"For the wages of sin is death." (Romans 6:23 HCSB).

Your good deeds will not be enough to overcome even one sin. One is enough to knock you completely out of God's boat forever. No matter how hard you work to earn salvation, it cannot be done. Brandon simply could not swim back to the boat on his own. He was bound for death unless someone stepped in to save him. We are like Brandon, returning to God in our own way will not happen; we need someone to save us.

REALIZE YOU NEED JESUS

Jesus died in our place, just like Jacob in the story. God sent His only Son, Jesus, to earth to be our sacrifice. When the Father in the story decided to throw the life buoy to Brandon, he sacrificed his very own son. It wasn't because He loved the son less, but because he loved the friend enough that he did not want him dying and going to Hell. God loved us enough that He sent His only Son to die for us. Jesus was willing to die because we were lost in sin. Because He died for us and defeated death, now Jesus is our life buoy.

Let's change this story again to fit my next point.

What if Brandon didn't grab the buoy! The Father would yell out, "Grab the life buoy! Do it now before it's too late, PLEASE! You will die if you don't grab onto this buoy! I let my own son die to save you, please don't do this!" But if Brandon refuses to grab the life buoy - he drowns. If he instead thinks he can swim back to the boat on his own – he drowns.

Hard to believe this story could get worse but it just did. The Father's sacrifice of his only son is not accepted, it was in vain. The Father allowed his only son to die so he could save Brandon, yet Brandon refused to accept it. It was his choice and he would not reach out for the life buoy.

That is exactly what happens when you allow some wrong belief about Jesus to keep you from being saved. Because of Jesus you are given a chance to grab life, real life, but you sometimes just let it go as you slowly die. Though God sends people in your path to tell you the good news of Jesus, for whatever reason, you refuse. Imagine how God feels when, after sacrificing His only Son, you don't choose to accept the sacrifice and when you die you live forever in Hell.

Because we have sinned just once, we can't be in God's presence in Heaven. That one sin of ours tossed us out of God's perfect boat. The waves of sin and death are too strong for us and we are being pulled away from God forever by the storm of death, just like both boys. Nothing will work except the Life Buoy, Jesus Christ.

BELIEVE THE LIFE BUOY CAN SAVE YOU

Like Brandon, you can't swim back to the boat. It's impossible. You have sinned and fallen short of the Glory of God. There is no way to get back to the boat, accept one, Jesus. You must believe that this life buoy, Jesus, will save you.

The life buoy the Father threw out to Brandon was a flotation device. Brandon had to believe this life buoy would hold him up and save him. That is faith. By faith he believed he wouldn't sink straight to the bottom when he grabbed it. You must believe the same thing about Jesus. You must believe that He can and will save you if you reach out to Him. And the best part is when you reach out to grab on to Jesus, He will hold on to you and never let go.

You can claim to know the buoy exists and look at it, talk about it, even tell others about it, yet still drown. You can get really close to the buoy and convince someone you grabbed it, yet sink to your death. You can say to yourself, "I will grab it later," but later never comes. If you want to be saved you must reach out and accept the free gift of Jesus. Believe He will save you, ask Him to do so, and allow Him to be Lord of your life.

Are you ready for question #1? Do you know your answer?

This is not a one-time invitation; it's a lifetime commitment. Your life is about to change forever and you will never regret it. Hit your knees and ask Jesus to save you and forgive your sins right now. Make Him Lord of your life.

A SAMPLE PRAYER TO HELP

This prayer alone will not save you. Your prayer must be a reflection of what is in your heart. You may use this prayer as a guide to accept Jesus now.

Jesus, I know I am a lost sinner drowning in this world separated from you. Jesus I can't save myself, so please save me. I am reaching out to you right now and ask you forgive me and come into my heart as Lord of my life. Thank you Jesus for saving me.

READY FOR THE NEXT STEP

If you just accepted Christ as your personal Savior you just changed the course of your future forever, for eternity! Jesus has breathed new life into you as a lifeguard on the beach resuscitates a drowning victim. Real life, both here and in Heaven, now is yours forever.

"Therefore, If anyone is in Christ, there is a new creation; Old things have passed away, and look, new things have come." (2 Corinthians 5:17 HCSB).

Your life has just changed and you are now a new person from the inside out. Your journey begins today. It will change you, your family and those around you. I hope this book will help you begin serving those around you as a hero to One.

CHAPTER 3. LEADING THEM TO JESUS

Why is it so important to be able to lead others to Jesus? You may think if you invite someone to church they will hear about Jesus and that will be good enough. Right? It wasn't good enough for Billy's friend, Josh. And it may not be good enough for your friend either. Yes, they may come to church and hear about Jesus, but will they respond? Maybe. Maybe not.

Suppose you become burdened for a lost friend at school and invite him to church. He shows up Sunday morning and the music is great. Sunday school class is nice topped off with cupcakes. You glance over to see if your friend is enjoying himself as much as you are. But his hands are buried deep in his pockets; you suspect he's not enjoying this as much as you are.

At school the next day you ask your friend, "Well, what did you think?" Hoping for a positive response you instead hear, "I don't think church is for me, but thanks anyway." You are devastated. This is where your efforts to bring your friend to Jesus end. You have no more ammo in your belt. At this point, you might give up - and many do.

I may have just described your latest adventure in connecting your friend with Jesus. If so, I have the answer for you: You did a fantastic job getting your friend to church, but you failed at getting Jesus to your friend.

You invited him to sing songs he'd never heard, pray to a God he doesn't know, and listen to a preacher discuss a book he hasn't read. No, he didn't really like church compared playing video games which he normally does on Sunday. You must be prepared to invite him to more than church; you must invite him to Jesus.

I am not suggesting we stop inviting friends to church. However, we can't put all our eggs in this one basket. Not everyone will respond to our church service. They may need a life-on-life experience of you telling them about Jesus on a personal basis. So keep inviting him to church, but don't let that be your final straw. You have much more to offer.

GETTING JESUS TO YOUR FRIEND

Our youth gave an evangelistic performance that combined drama, music and interpretive movement. We called it Interpadrama. In this performance, I told a story about two high school girls. The fictitious characters were Rachael, a Christian, and Barrett, her lost friend.

In the story, Rachael was too shy to tell Barrett about Jesus and how He could save her. Sound familiar? However, Rachael was worried that Barrett did not know Jesus. One day, Rachael persuaded Barrett to attend a Wednesday night youth event. The topic was Fatherly Love. Barrett had been through several stepfathers over the course of a few short years. Many of them had either physically or mentally abused her and her mom.

As they were leaving the church, Barrett broke down in tears. "Rachael I don't understand what the youth minister meant when he said God loves us like a father. All my fathers have hated me." Barrett had never experienced fatherly love at all, so it did not make any sense to her.

They sat down on the front steps of the church as Barrett poured her heart out about her life and how she wished she could know true fatherly love. Rachael knew this was an open door for her to talk about Jesus. Yet she sat quietly. Fear of saying the wrong thing kept her quiet. After several minutes of silence, Barrett stood up, walked to her car and drove home.

Rachael knew she had missed another chance to tell her friend about Jesus. She was just too scared to do it. Rachael needed to overcome her fear of witnessing before it was too late. But she decided maybe next time she could do it. But next time may not come.

At 3:33 a.m. that same night Rachael received a call that Barrett was in the hospital. When Rachael arrived at the ER the paramedic met her in the lobby with the news. "Barrett is in a coma and may not live through the night. When she arrived home a little bit late her mother's drunken boyfriend beat her, threw her down a flight of stairs, causing massive brain trauma."

Rachael opened the door to Barrett's ICU room. It was dark except for the small light in the corner. Only the slow, repetitive beeps of the monitor broke a dead silence. Her friend clung to life, only a few breaths away from eternity. Rachael hit her knees: "God give me one more chance. Don't let her die."

Was it too late for this prayer? Was it too late for Rachael to tell Barrett about Jesus? Was it too late for Barrett?

Imagine yourself right now in that hospital room on your knees. Would you feel like Rachael? Would you too beg for another chance?

Barrett's clock was ticking. Her test was about to end and she didn't have the right answer to question #1. Rachael did not know her opportunity to witness to Barrett at the Church might be her last. Rachael missed her Divine Appointment to witness and now it was too late.

In this story, God set it up so Rachael could witness to Barrett but she didn't do it and Barrett paid the price. How will you answer the call? Will you be a witness for Jesus before it is too late for someone you love?

WHAT A TREAT!

When you lead another person to Jesus Christ you are in for a life treat! The feeling of leading someone to faith in Jesus Christ, knowing their eternal destination changed before your eyes, is the biggest blessing this side of your own salvation. I never tire of watching others come to Jesus and seeing their reaction. So you want to learn how? The most important thing is to know it's not as complicated as we make it out to be. You must understand God is at work all around you...so go join Him!

CHAPTER 4. SALVATION: START TO FINISH

In our understanding of how salvation works, we must first start with the power source, God. Suppose Lilly got up this morning and decided to lead her friend to Jesus. Lilly told Hannah about Jesus and before the bell rang she fell to her knees and came to saving faith in Jesus. Would Lilly think the credit goes to her for getting up and deciding to do this? Would she say, "I saved my friend today because finally I woke up and cared enough to do so." No because God must be working or no one gets saved.

Without the power source, God, salvation does not happen. Therefore, if Lilly can't take credit for her friend accepting Jesus, she can't take blame for the ones who reject.

You must understand now – it is not up to you whether someone accepts or rejects Jesus.

TEN STEPS OF SALVATION

I believe the Bible gives us clear steps to how salvation takes place in each of our lives. These steps happen in sequence and may happen within minutes or take months or years. Let's begin.

STEP 1: PRAYER

Nothing happens without prayer. We are instructed to pray for those we want to see come to Jesus. If you are trying to lead your friend to Jesus and nothing else works, try prayer. Unless our mission is bathed in prayer, we are battling against the odds. It's like picking up a radio and plugging it into the wall; prayer makes that connection to the power source of salvation.

About six months before our youth mission trip to Brunswick, Georgia in 2005, we began praying as a group for those whom we would meet. Our focus was to see people saved or plant seeds that would one day grow into salvation. Church members took turns coming to our youth meetings specifically to pray for this very thing.

Each week we spent time in prayer asking God to soften the hearts of those we would meet on the trip. We prayed the gospel message would be heard and understood. The months of prayer prior to our trip set the stage for everything else that happened. Without prayer we would be doing this under our own power.

PRAYING FOR THE LOST

I have often been told to be careful what I pray for, as I may get it. Prayer is just that way. We need to be very specific about our prayers because...God answers them! Since we are learning how God works in salvation it makes sense to follow the right path in our prayers for the lost. We must first pray for the release of the lost soul from its captor, Satan.

Satan has blinded your lost friends making it nearly impossible for them to understand the gospel. Unless the person is set free, he will not see Jesus. I can't set anyone free and neither can you, but the Holy Spirit can. Let's look at what scripture says about the blinded souls around us.

"Satan, who is the god of this world, has blinded the minds of those who don't believe. They are unable to see the glorious light of the good news." (II Corinthians 4:4 NLT)

Paul, in the scripture above, was talking about the good news of Jesus Christ and why some did not see the light. It wasn't Paul's fault. Likewise, it isn't your fault or your preacher's fault some do not see the light. It is the fault of the one who has blinded them, Satan. So, we must pray for their release from Satan's bond long enough that they can consider the Gospel. Every lost person may appear normal on the outside, but in the spiritual world they are chained, blindfolded and bound, and don't even know it.

SATAN THE CAPTOR

Have you ever watched a movie about a hostage crisis? Did you notice the hostage is almost always blindfolded? Why do captors blindfold their captives? Well, I have a hunch that in the Kidnapping for Dummies handbook, it's on page one. It makes the hostage dependent upon the kidnapper. Do you know who else read, Kidnapping for Dummies? You guessed it, Satan. He is prepared to blind anyone from the powerful light of Jesus so they become completely dependent upon him.

During most hostage movies, the negotiator rolls in and takes over. He negotiates with the kidnapper in many different and creative ways, such as the one-hostage-for-one-pizza swap. The main thing the negotiator tries to do is build trust and play on any goodness that may exist in the heart of the kidnapper. The negotiator will try to make the kidnapper believe there is a way out, some type of hope. As long as there is hope, the kidnapper may not pull the trigger.

Spiritual hostages held by Satan face a much worse fate. No good resides within Satan. There will not be any hostage swaps for pizzas. Satan knows there will be no leniency with God as Judge on that final day. So Satan has no reason to negotiate because he knows there is no hope for him. He wants to take us all to Hell with him. Scripture clearly shows us the state of Satan's attitude toward us:

"Stay alert! Watch out for your great enemy, the devil. He prowls around like a roaring lion, looking for someone to devour." (I Peter 5:8 NLT)

If we can't negotiate, what do we do? Pray! It's the only weapon that works every time it's tried. Below is a sample prayer you can use when praying for your lost friend. Just fill in the blank with his or her name.

SAMPLE PRAYER FOR THE LOST

Lord, I ask you to be with _____, draw an invisible circle and keep out the influence of Satan. Set him free. Lord, touch his heart. Convict _____ that his sin has separated him from You. Lord, I pray you will open his heart and eyes. Let him see your light and understand the truth. Lord, allow me or someone else to have a Divine Appointment with him so we can share Jesus. Amen

You do not have to follow this prayer exactly. However, there are four parts to this prayer I believe are very important and should be included when praying for the lost.

PART 1: SET FREE FROM SATAN

Notice in the first part of the prayer you are asking your friend to be set free from Satan. This is necessary so that God can draw a circle around your friend and allow you to share Jesus with him. If you are praying for a mission trip just pray for anyone He draws into your path.

Are you a Star Wars fan? Remember how a force field protects the starship from enemy lasers? The lasers bounce right off. We want God putting that same kind of spiritual force field around the lost person so Satan can't blind him while you are witnessing. Satan does not want him to hear the words you share about Jesus. When you pray that God will shield your friend God separates him from Satan's influence long enough for you or someone else to witness.

In Star Wars, Luke Skywalker could only fight and defeat Darth Vader when the force was strong with him. Luke trained for months learning how to use the force for good. Without it he would be no match for the dark side. Star Wars is science fiction but the battle between good and evil is not. We are fighting a battle against evil and need the help of the Holy Spirit. This rescue of your friend from evil is called sanctification, one of those churchy words that means God is separating your friend from the world to belong to God.

PART 2: FEELING CONVICTION

The prayer next asks God to convict the heart of your friend so he will feel the conviction of his sin in order to repent. Later in this book we will talk about feeling conviction for sin.

PART 3: UNDERSTANDING THE GOSPEL

Your prayer next includes that God will give him understanding of the Gospel and open his eyes to see the light. We will have a section later on Understanding the Gospel.

PART 4: DIVINE APPOINTMENT

The last part of the prayer is asking God for a Divine Appointment. Divine Appointments are moments in time set aside by God so you or someone else may share the Gospel. Divine appointments will be discussed in depth in a later chapter and are very important to witnessing.

The four major parts of your prayer should be:

1: Set him free.

2: Convict his heart.

3: Give him understanding and open his eyes to the Gospel.

4: Give you or someone a Divine Appointment to share Christ.

DOES THIS PRAYER GUARANTEE SALVATION?

Will Jesus respond to our salvation prayers? Absolutely!
Will He take the person to the edge of salvation and invite
him to eternal life? Yes, He will! Will He force the person to
get saved? No He will not.

God may swing the jail bars wide open but he won't force the
prisoner to escape.

Here is an example. My youth and I focused this very prayer
on Laura. Laura told us she was an atheist - one who doesn't
believe God exists. We used the sample prayer above and
began praying regularly for her.

Amazingly, soon after we began praying she agreed to come
to our youth meetings and even participated in an
interpretive movement during church service. She was
enjoying it and we were able to witness to her every time she
came. Eventually she found herself standing on the edge of
decision. God drew a circle of protection around her and
removed the blindfold long enough to allow us to witness.
God swung open the gates and only one thing separated her
from Jesus, her surrender.

We could tell she was under the conviction of the Holy Spirit.
Yet, just as she was getting close to the making a decision
about Jesus, she pulled away. She ran back into her jail cell
slamming the bars shut behind her. She eventually stopped
responding to our invites to church and to talk about Jesus.
She moved away after graduation and we have not seen her
since.

Did we feel defeated? You bet we did. In the eyes of God, were we defeated? Not at all! We did exactly what the Word of God calls us to do. We prayed for her, we witnessed to her and we loved her.

I believe there will be a time that she may accept Jesus as her Savior. That the seeds we were allowed to plant may grow and set her free. But for now, we must have the away team perspective. We must continue to pray for her and know one day a victory may come.

We must care enough to pray for our lost friends or strangers we hope to meet. Do not let Satan win by forgetting the importance of step #1 of the salvation process. Don't make the mistake so many made in Star Wars by taking on the dark side without the force being with them. We cannot and should not try to take on Satan and his demons without the help of God through prayer.

At this very moment someone you know has been taken hostage. They are blindfolded and there will be no negotiation. Their only hope is in Christ. How will you respond? Will you care enough today to pray for the release your lost friend?

STEP 2: GOD DRAWS THEM

Jesus said:

"No one can come to Me unless the Father who sent Me draws him." (John 6:44 HCSB)

IF WE ARE SAVED, WE ARE SENT

Paul Continued:

"And how will anyone go and tell them without being sent? That is why the Scriptures say, 'How beautiful are the feet of messengers who bring good news!'" (Romans 10:15 NLT)

If we are saved, we are sent to be messengers of the good news. We may be sent to our friend in class, to a relative in another state or to another country. What an amazing job to have! And to top it all off, if you carry the good news to others you have beautiful feet. I've never been accused of having beautiful feet but I accept the compliment.

THE HOLY SPIRIT IS YOUR GUIDE

One day, my eight-year-old daughter Jenna, wanted to drive my truck down the driveway. I reluctantly agreed. She climbed in my lap and we took off. At first, I had my hands on the wheel to help her steer around the curves. After the second curve I took my hands off the wheel and she drove straight into the yard. "DADDY!" she yelled. As if it was my fault. I said, "You are driving, not me darling."

"But you helped the first time," she argued. She was expecting me to continue to steer the truck around the tough corners. "Look," I said. "Do you want to just sit in my lap or do you want to drive?" She answered, "drive."

So Jenna crawled back in my lap and I moved my hand to the bottom of the steering wheel. As we began moving again, I would barely touch the wheel and help guide it in the direction we should go. My hand was out of the way so she could not see it. I didn't do the driving, but instead made sure she was turning in the right direction. This gave her more freedom to turn the wheel; and she paid a lot more attention to the curves. With my hand guiding the direction we went, she started learning how to drive.

Even though I wasn't doing the driving, she was glad to know I had my hand there. It gave her comfort to know that if she veered off course I would lightly touch the wheel in the direction she should go. It also taught her to be very careful and pay attention to the wheel. If she grabbed the wheel and turned it hard in the wrong direction, she would never feel my slight touch on the wheel.

The Holy Spirit works in much the same way when we witness. The Holy Spirit may help direct you when you witness to your friend. The Spirit may place on your heart things to say. But, the Holy Spirit will not overcome you if you are determined to work on your own. If you grab the conversation and take over without being careful to listen to the Spirit, you may cause a train wreck. You must be patient so you can feel those subtle turns the Spirit may make. Isn't it awesome to know we can control the wheel of witnessing, yet still have help!

Could Jenna still run off the road if she was not careful? Of course. How else could she learn unless there were consequences to her actions? When we witness, even though the Holy Spirit is with us, we can still mess things up. We are human and will drive right into the ditch sometimes.

I used Jenna's driving mistake as a teaching moment for her. She experienced how much care she needed to take in steering the truck, or we would go off course. It made her more aware of her responsibility. Could it be that God may use our little mess-ups as teaching moments? I believe He does.

Although we may make a mess of things, it doesn't necessarily mean the Holy Spirit did not work in the heart of the lost person and in teaching you. Even though we sometimes think what we say did not come out just right, the Holy Spirit has a way of making things positive. Does this give you permission to drive straight off a bridge and be careless in what you say? No! We must do everything possible to prepare for witnessing. But learning to witness comes through experience, just like driving.

Is Jenna now ready to go get the milk and eggs from the grocery by herself at age 8? She would say yes, but...NO! That is why she will slowly learn how to drive and I will be there to guide her. In the same way, our ability to lead someone to Christ is dependent upon how much we prepare ourselves and listen to the Holy Spirit.

LESS STUFF IS MORE JESUS

Our youth mission trip to Georgia had finally arrived. After months of praying we found ourselves in Perry Park located deep in a poverty stricken area in Brunswick, Georgia. Our way of attracting kids to the park was to give a performance based on the recent Star Wars III movie. We featured Darth Vader, Anakin and Yoda; the rest of the youth were Jedi

Knights equipped with their own light sabers and capes. We included light saber battles and training for the kids.

Participants made their own racing pods out of large boxes and held a race. We had games, prizes and cool stuff to give away. The Gospel was delivered at the end, connected to the story of Star Wars, good versus evil. It was sure to win the hearts of those lost kids; or so we thought.

When we arrived at Perry Park, it was 100 degrees with no kids in sight. We were told that if we started playing games the kids would show up. That advice worked well. We set up our band equipment, played music, displayed our games and prizes and staked out a spot for our pod race. Everywhere we looked we found broken glass from beer bottles and the kids were showing up in droves...barefoot!

We finally cleared an area where the race could be conducted and donned our costumes. More kids arrived and to say they were misbehaving would be an understatement. They were breaking our games, throwing our equipment and stealing our prizes. I had never seen this much disrespect from such small kids. It was obvious the hours we had spent preparing the games and learning our performance was not going to work. We couldn't even get started with our first game because kids were so out of control. I had to make a decision on what we would do and I wanted to leave. How could we share Jesus if we couldn't even keep them calm long enough to give away prizes?

Brian, my assistant youth minister, and I discussed what to do next. I told him things were about to change but I didn't know how. We then knelt down and prayed as the chaos ensued.

As we finished praying God did an amazing thing. We felt swallowed up by God's presence, like being inside a bubble. I felt protected from everything and it became clear what I must do.

I walked to the microphone and got everyone's attention; which needless to say took some time. Kids were still running around yelling and destroying our equipment and cursing at us. Finally, they quieted and listened to what I had to say.

"We came a long way to play with you, to sing to you, to give you gifts and prizes, but your disrespect has stopped us. We came to do all this so we could tell you about Jesus. My team will now put away every game, every prize, and the sound equipment. The party is over."

At this point, the kids grew silent. Pointing to the far end of the park I continued, "I am going under that big shade tree and I plan to stand there and tell the true story of Jesus. No more games, no more prizes, nothing will be given away. If you want to hear about Jesus, follow me. If not, we have nothing else to offer you and this event is over."

I turned to walk to the big shade tree and could feel every eye on me. I felt so stupid and it was eerily quiet. As I walked toward the tree by myself I fully expected a huge round of laughter from those little demons to burst out at any moment.

I thought, "Ok God, I will get over here by the tree and be standing alone and look so silly." I was trying to think of my next move once I reached the tree. Maybe crawl up into a little ball or pretend to search for acorns? Or hide behind the tree and talk to myself? I simply didn't want to turn around when I reached the shade tree in fear of what I might see. I fully expected to be there alone and then have to pack up and go to the motel in defeat.

As I reached the shade tree, I took a deep breath and turned around. To my surprise twelve of those rowdy kids had stopped playing, put down their "stolen" prizes and followed me to the tree. I could not believe it! How could a group of out of control, screaming, cursing, and disrespectful kids suddenly change in seconds? Kids who were too rowdy to run a race were now choosing to sit down and here a story about Jesus. How could this be?

GOD. God did that with His power. Nothing more, nothing less. It was clear God had drawn them, not Star Wars.

WHAT IF WE DIDN'T PRAY?

Had Brian and I not prayed I would have implemented my plan to ask my team to load up and leave. I would tell my group we tried our best. In my speech later that evening, I would have said we gave those scoundrels a chance to have a good time and hear a little about Jesus, but they didn't listen. We never would have talked about Perry Park again. End of story.

But two things happened in the course of about 1 minute. We prayed, and we listened. Seems simple, but it was hard to do for me. All our ideas, hard work and practice just got crushed by a bunch of rowdy kids. I wanted to let pride take over and leave. But God moved so powerfully in my heart I couldn't walk away and neither could the group, so we stayed.

I sometimes wonder how many Perry Parks I have walked away from without seeking God's will first. It was the Holy Spirit slightly touching the wheel of my heart in the direction we should go. We would not have felt that subtle tug to change direction had we not hit our knees and prayed.

KEEP IT SIMPLY JESUS

Scattered around me in a circle at the big tree was my youth praying, crying, anticipating. Without being told my youth group had spread across the park praying and witnessing. Under that shade tree I told the story of Jesus from the moment sin entered the world in the Garden of Eden to the Cross. As I spoke, kids and some parents walked up to hear God's Word.

God and nothing else drew them. Prayer had released them from their captor, Satan. A rather large crowd gathered around us in Perry Park. The park had turned from chaos to a sanctuary around that old shade tree.

The kids who had been causing the most trouble went inside the tennis courts and threw rocks and sticks at us as we taught Jesus. I truly believe Angels were surrounding us that day and protecting us from harm. It was as if God took the ones who were bent on causing others not to listen and put them inside the cage of the tennis court.

He then opened the hearts of those who would listen, and they listened intently! I've never witnessed such as change in attitude.

After completing the story of Jesus, I gave an invitation and several hands went up. These kids wanted to know more about this Jesus who could save them. The youth quickly grabbed raised hands and moved to private places all over the park so they could personally witness to them.

After about an hour of witnessing and praying with many kids, the feeling around us changed. In our hearts, God seemed to say, "Ok, your work is done, you need to leave." I felt the presence of evil again and the people who were gathering now in the park did not seem friendly. We loaded up quickly and got all the youth in the van as it was becoming dangerous with the crowd gathering in the park.

As I came to the church van, one of my youth ran up and said, "Stop, there is one more kid who wants to know Jesus."

There, standing on the court, was a boy with a basketball in his hand. I could tell by his face the Holy Spirit had convicted him as he stared at us...waiting. It was obvious my youth had already told him the story of Jesus and how to be saved.

He and I knelt on that hot asphalt; ball players stopped to see what was going on as this boy prayed to receive Jesus as his personal Savior. As we stood up, I will never forget the sight of my youth peering out the van windows. Their tear covered faces pressed against the glass. Each had witnessed God at work that day and they knew it.

As we tried to leave we had to stop twice to pull kids off our church van. They clung to our bumper. Pulling those kids off our van remains fresh in my mind. Only two hours before, they were calling us names. Now, they begged us to stay. Why? Because they saw a glimpse of something real: the love of Jesus.

As we drove away, we could only weep. Kids chased our van down the street to wave good-bye one last time. As the last kid disappeared behind us, my eyes drifted to the rearview mirror. Fourteen tear filled faces with torn hearts filled the seats of our van.

We were overwhelmed by the power God displayed in transforming those kids. Satan's playground had been turned into God's sanctuary and we had front row seats. As we drove away it was clear we had not performed a block party, we had experienced God! Jesus saved ten kids and one adult that day at Perry Park and changed most of us forever.

WHAT JESUS TAUGHT AT PERRY PARK

It is so clear what Jesus taught us that day. Our work, time and resources had gone into preparing this elaborate performance and games. These games were designed to attract the kids and it was our intent to spend about two hours at the park with only 30 minutes dedicated to the sharing of the Gospel. Jesus made it clear that day to forget all we had prepared and simply talk about Him, to trust Him more to draw the kids.

We had been told Perry Park would be a difficult place to go and many groups who came there avoided that area. They told us the kids were used to church groups showing up, playing games and giving away gifts. They knew the routine and we were no different. Until God changed the plan.

At Perry Park, all the other steps had been completed. The kids had been prayed for; God had drawn them and prepared their hearts. It was now time to tell the good news. Like Paul said, how could they believe in Jesus unless they heard about Him?

The games would not accomplish God's plan as we would have rushed through the Gospel due to time constraints. I am so glad the Holy Spirit touched the wheel and directed us slightly in the direction we should go. I'm glad we just slowed down and shared Jesus.

Our lesson that day? Less stuff is more Jesus. Those kids simply needed to know why Jesus came and died for them. They needed to know who Jesus is and that He loved them and could save them from Hell. They didn't need all the games and prizes that they had been given all year long by other groups. They needed something different, something real.

Sometimes you just need to tell them about Jesus. Part three of hearing the Gospel would not have been accomplished if we had walked away. You won't need a six member band in the school hallway to lead worship before you share Jesus with your friend. You don't need your pastor to join you in math class. Just talk to your friend about Jesus.

Telling the story of Jesus led to the next step of salvation, the wonderful gift of faith.

STEP 4: GIFT OF FAITH, THE POWER TO BELIEVE

It would be nice to say that my telling of the story of Jesus was so powerful that day at Perry Park that those lost kids were just begging for forgiveness. My perfectly constructed words caused Heaven to touch Earth spilling out a fury of salvations all over the place. My powerful words drove faith into the hearts of those lost kids like driving a stake into the heart of a vampire. Don't you wish you could do such a job as I?

Wait! Don't delete or toss away this book yet I'm only joking around to make a point. I know my words were not the reason those kids came to Jesus. I only played the small part of being there and talking about Jesus. It wasn't that any of us said the perfect things in a perfect way that finally gave them faith in Jesus. But you know what? How many times have you been too afraid to share Jesus with a friend after you thought, "What if I say the wrong thing?"

Follow me down this road for a block or two. If you think you could say the wrong thing and cause someone to not have faith, then would saying the right thing gave them faith? Believing you could "mess up" also means you could "succeed" as well. I believe this wrong belief is what causes the most fear in sharing about Jesus. News flash - you are not in control of whether your friend has faith.

I totally understand what you may think because I once thought this way: "What if I say the wrong thing and mess up and I get confused and that person walks away and dies and goes to Hell all because I said the wrong thing! Yikes!! Get me out of here fast!" So, in fear of saying the wrong thing, you say nothing. Sound familiar at all? If so, don't miss this next point.

Whether or not someone places faith in Jesus is totally out of your hands. Yes, you can relax. You have nothing to do with someone developing faith in Jesus. The good news, Faith is a gift from God, not from you.

We are not born with faith to believe in Jesus. That is given to us by God the Father at the moment we hear God's Word. It is a free gift from God and we are all given the same amount of faith to believe. You don't have to know everything about the Bible - only the truth of Jesus.

"For by grace you have been saved through faith, and that not of yourselves, it is the gift of God." (Ephesians 2:8 HCSB)

There are two separate issues at work here: God giving us faith to believe, and the act of believing. The faith to believe is a gift from God; making the decision to believe is our choice. You and I share Jesus with a friend, God gives the faith, and our friend chooses to believe or not. Isn't it amazing! Not only did Jesus die on the Cross but He also gives us the faith we need to believe it. Now that's Amazing Grace!

OUR FATHER GIVES IT TO US

Jenna recently came to me with a compassionate heart. She explained her desire to donate money to St. Luke Children's Hospital in Memphis, TN. She asked if I would give her money so she could donate. I thought, "Isn't that like me donating and not you?" She's really good at getting me to do things so she can take credit. I guess it's a daughter father kind of thing.

At school, they had told the students about St. Luke's Children's Hospital and the heart-wrenching stories of those kids with cancer who needed our help and donations. She wanted to respond by donating money. The problem? She didn't have money to donate. So she went to the one she knew would have money and would give it to her so she could donate, her father.

We do the same thing with God. We hear the story of Jesus and we want to respond, but we simply don't have the faith. That's Ok, we have a Father in Heaven who will give us the faith we need in order to believe in Him. I simply didn't have any faith until God gave it to me. Then, armed with that faith, I chose to believe. How great is that!

STEP 5: MENTALLY UNDERSTAND THE GOSPEL

We must understand the Gospel and what it means to our life. Studies show it takes on average over seven times to hear the Gospel before someone accepts Jesus in their heart. For some, the first listen is all it takes to mentally understand the gospel; for others, it may take longer. But to accept Jesus as our personal Savior, we must understand mentally what that means.

This will be why some may want to ask questions or even take time to think about this decision. Everyone is different in how they understand and decide what they will do with

Jesus. So be patient and love them like Jesus as they make their decision. Even if it takes months of sharing be patient. Otherwise, your impatience may cause them to shy away.

I was in a very large gymnasium with hundreds of kids of all ages sitting on the floor. We had watched a really cool juggling performance and now the performer was sharing Jesus. At the end he shared how to accept Jesus as Savior. Asking for a show of hands he said, "How many of you want to go to Heaven?" Naturally every kid in the gym raised their hand, including me! Nobody wants to go to Hell.

With hands raised all over the gym floor he led everyone in an audible prayer to accept Jesus and be saved. Did two hundred kids in that gym suddenly come to faith in Jesus? It could happen, but only if they mentally understood what they were doing. Were they convicted of their sins and committing themselves to Jesus or simply signing up for a free ticket out of Hell?

Was Savannah thinking, "Hey I will raise my hand and go to Heaven, why not?" Was Allie raising her hand because Charleigh did? Was Anna in because Jeff was in? Does this matter? I believe it does. We must mentally understand the Gospel and be convicted of our sin before we can turn from it and come to Jesus. We don't just simply sign up for Heaven, we must commit to Jesus and make Him our Lord and Savior.

This is why you may encounter a friend at school that simply has never heard much about Jesus. Don't let him think you are signing him up for a field trip. When you witness to him remember asking if he wants to stay out of Hell isn't the proper question. We don't want to scare our friends away from Hell. We want to love them toward Jesus.

Hell was not created to scare us toward Jesus. It was created for Satan and the other demons and we only go there if we refuse to accept Jesus as our Savior. Sell your friends on Jesus not on a ticket out of Hell.

AGE OF ACCOUNTABILITY

Mentally understanding the Gospel is very important especially when witnessing to very young people. Why? The age of accountability is in play. I believe there is an age when a young person finally becomes mentally capable of understanding the good news of Jesus. It may be five years old for a few and older for others. When they mentally understand the Gospel they are then able to either reject or accept Jesus. This moment becomes their age of accountability and beyond that point their test has begun.

Once this person reaches this age of accountability they will need to accept Jesus as their Savior in order to go to Heaven upon death. In the gym that night there were many kids with raised hands that probably had not reached the mental understanding of Jesus. Yet the performer pronounced them saved if they recited the prayer. Scripture doesn't back that up. We must accept Jesus as our Savior when we mentally understand and we must do it ourselves, not by repeating a prayer led by a juggler.

The age of accountability belief comes from Scripture in the Old Testament. I take you back to King David in 2nd Samuel.

His son was very sick. He prayed God would spare his son's life but his son died at a very young age.

David's advisers were amazed that while his child was still alive David cried and prayed and would not eat. But after his son died he stopped crying, cleaned up and began to eat. This is how David responded.

"I fasted and wept while the child was alive, for I said 'Perhaps the Lord will be gracious to me and let the child live.' But why should I fast when he is dead? Can I bring him back again? I will go to him one day, but he cannot return to me." (2 Samuel 12:22-23 NLT)

David says, "I will go to him one day." David fully expected to see his child in Heaven one day. I believe this is the same for all children who have not reached the age of accountability.

They will go to Heaven if they die before this age of accountability. Therefore, you may witness to a young person who has not reached his ability to understand the Gospel and may agree to anything you ask them about going to Heaven. So be sure the person you are witnessing to, if very young, is mentally understanding the Gospel before moving to the prayer of salvation.

If you have been witnessing to someone who is very young and you are not sure if they truly understand the Gospel take your time. Enlist the help of another Christian. Just make sure they mentally understand the good news of Jesus.

STEP 6: EMOTIONALLY FEEL SORROW FOR SIN

When I catch Jenna doing something wrong, she normally reacts with sorrow. However, she is sorry she got caught more than the fact that she did something wrong. Emotional sorrow for our sin is not that we got caught, but that we realize who we are in the presence of God. This emotional sorrow is when we realize we are separated from God because of sin and we can't save ourselves. We see ourselves as sinners and that it was our sin Jesus died for on the Cross.

I watched Jenna go through this very stage at age eight when she came to know the Lord. She sat in our Sunday School class for about 30 minutes with tears running down her face and totally speechless. I would ask a question but she could not answer. She was feeling emotional sorrow and her reaction was easy to recognize. Not everyone reacts the same way so do not think a very emotional reaction is needed during this part of the salvation process.

This emotional sorrow is not the same as being sorry you sinned. Judas was sorry he had sinned against Jesus when he betrayed Him. Judas, after seeing the treatment of Jesus, ran back to the chief priests and threw that blood money on the floor, demanding they let Jesus go.

But, despite him being sorry for what he had done, he hung himself and never sought forgiveness from Jesus. (The story of Judas betraying Jesus can be found in Matthew chapter 26)

Godly sorrow for our sin brings us to a point of repentance, a turning away from that sin which takes us to the next step.

STEP 7: CHOOSE TO BELIEVE

Look at the path the lost person has traveled to this point: Your prayers, God drawing them, the Gospel presented, faith was given by God, mental understanding and Godly sorrow overwhelmed them. Now the lost person stands at the very edge of belief.

Have you seen the movie Indiana Jones and the Last Crusade? If not, it's worth watching. Pay close attention to the last moments of the film and relate everything that happens to how we come to Jesus.

Until you see the film I will do my best to explain the movie's last sequence of events. Indiana is going through a cave in search of the Holy Grail. After an incredible journey, Indy is close to finding what he has searched for almost all his life.

Indiana's father had put together a journal through years of study that detailed very specific instructions on how to proceed through the cave without being killed by the booby traps. After avoiding these death traps by following closely his Father's book, Indiana came to the final challenge.

Between him and the room holding the Holy Grail was a bottomless pit. There was no bridge; yet it was too far to jump. He stood with no options other than to turn back or go forward. Under his breath he said, "this is impossible, no one can jump this far!"

Looking again at his father's journal, it was clear Indy must take his next step into thin air. In the journal, his father had drawn a man stepping out over the bottomless pit with nothing to hold him up. To reach the Holy Grail, Indy would have to take a step solely on faith. He had to believe that his Father's book was true and correct.

I suppose that about this time, Indiana was thinking, "Ok father, I believe what you wrote in this book is true. The only way to get to the Holy Grail is if I believe enough to walk on thin air. But now that I believe, can I have a bridge? Is there another way I might be able to get to the Holy Grail? Maybe a back door that is much easier?"

The answer would be like that concerning salvation: No Indy, you must trust what the book says, you must take a step of faith. Just because he believes that this book is right doesn't get him to his prize. He will have to step out in faith and show he believes what the book says.

Indy breathes deeply, holds the journal to his heart and steps into thin air. As his foot comes down he lands on an invisible bridge. He looks at his feet, completely amazed that a bridge had caught him. All it took was that leap of faith; that step forward. He was then able to cross over to the other side to find the Holy Grail. What an excellent picture of what happens at this stage of salvation, choosing to believe.

The lost person now stands at the edge of decision - turn back or leap forward? Show faith or walk away? Step into the unknown or go back to the known? No words will save him, no act or deed will bridge the gap, only faith in action, the act of believing in the unseen.

The same is true with Jesus. We must accept and believe that which we can't see. It's so much more than realizing He may exist. Many have stood at this point in their life and actually believed Jesus was real, but never gave their life to Christ. They never truly trusted Jesus enough to say, "I want you to have all of me and save me and be Lord of my life."

It's required that we put our life in His hands through faith. When Indiana stepped out, he laid his life on the line believing he would not fall to his death. He believed his Father's book was real and true.

When we accept Jesus as our Savior, we take a leap of faith that He will save us and take care of us into eternity. We believe our Father's book, the Bible, is real and true. He saves us through the very faith that He gave us. We have stepped out and He will catch us every time. We chose to believe with the free gift of faith.

"For God loved the world so much that he gave his one and only Son, so that everyone who believes in Him will not perish but have eternal life." (John 3:16 NLT)

WHY WALK AWAY NOW?

Unfortunately, many come to this place only to walk away. I have seen many get to this point only to decide not to get saved. How can they walk away from eternal life? I ask that as if I never walked away. I rejected Jesus until I was twelve years old. Most of us have this opinion of lost people. We think, "Why won't they come to Christ! Don't they know what they are missing?"

No, they don't know what they are missing! I didn't know what I was missing until after I came to Jesus. We get scared, we believe a lie, then for whatever reason we turn and walk away.

There are many reasons the lost turn back from this leap of faith. But one reason may be a lack of understanding how His grace can be so amazing and require so little from us. Many think there must be more than just having faith in Jesus Christ as Lord of your life.

DO I NEED MORE THAN FAITH?

Have you ever watched the old TV show, Deal or No Deal? I've seen it once. On this particular episode, a lady was offered a chance to be given more than $500,000, if she would only kiss a frog and accept the deal. Her chances of winning a million were slim to none, but half of it sat on the table. She chose no deal. I couldn't believe it! What! Kiss the frog lady!

Growing up in the country, I kissed frogs in my normal course of daily playtime. Five bucks would have been enough for me. As a kid from rural Kentucky, when a big toad hopped nearby, I picked it up. I'd toss it around a while, and probably end up kissing it at some point. Maybe it was a big deal for the toad, but not for me.

I was puzzled to see the contestant walk away from easy money, which was her purpose for going on the show in the first place. I tried to figure out her thought process. She told the game show host she wanted a new house, wanted to pay for her second wedding and put her kid through college. Well, what do you know, the money she was offered along with a quick taste of live frog was at her fingertips; yet she passed it up.

Why?

I think the offer was so huge and the task so small she thought the dealer was trying to trick her. She was offered around $270,000; the deal would double if she would kiss Mr. Froggy. I believe she thought that was too much for such a simple act. Therefore, it just can't be, the odds must be in her favor, so she passed it up.

Many times, the lost stand at the edge of forgiveness, understanding their sin and how it has separated them from God. They believe He died for them and that Jesus is real. Yet they simply can't believe that all their sins can be forgiven without their part being harder. They simply can't understand this amazing grace. It's too easy for their part when compared to the enormous price Jesus paid on the Cross.

But that's the point; Jesus paid it all. With all the awful things they have done in life, all the times they ran from God and broke his commandments, here they stand, being offered Heaven simply for believing and accepting Jesus as their personal Savior. And they don't even have to kiss a frog!

Satan convinces some that they are simply unforgivable. So the person stands there convinced of who Jesus is; yet not believing grace is free. They think they are not good enough to become a Christian. They just walk away and say "no deal." If they never return to this spot, they will die and receive nothing but Hell. There will not be a better deal offered.

Don't Forget What It's Like to be Lost

Let me make a point about the frog. I forget what it was like to have never kissed a frog. Likewise we should not forget what it was like to be lost.

As I said earlier, I would kiss a frog for almost any amount of money. Even though kissing the frog was a no-brainer for many of the viewers, it's also possible she had never kissed a frog before - most haven't. If she had never experienced her first frog kiss, she was probably much more reluctant to do so, especially in front of millions of viewers.

Maybe she thought it would be much harder to kiss a frog than it really is. I would guess my first time to plant one on a frog was a dare situation with a buddy. Maybe I hesitated as well.

It would be odd to be offered $270,000 to kiss a frog. I suppose it would make you wonder how awful this experience must be for that kind of money.

Likewise, we forget what it was like to be lost and to make that huge decision of stepping out into the unknown. Now that we are on this side, we think people must be crazy not to accept Christ. We forget what it was like to stand at the edge of that divide, knowing a huge gulf separated us from God.

That first step of faith as a lost person doesn't come easily or naturally. It really is hard, it really is a big step forward, and we must remember that so we don't lose our patience with those standing on the edge of decision. Don't be pushy. If you push them off the cliff toward salvation, it's not an act of faith on their part. Instead, love them like Jesus and be patient.

When you are witnessing and your friend is standing on the edge of decision, you need to know two things:

1) God has given each of us free will to choose Him. She may walk away.

2) If she walks away, she rejects Jesus, not you.

So do not take it personally and do not give up on her. Continue to do work to bring them back to this place.

Remember! If you treat the person with respect when they turn and walk away from the edge of decision, then you may have another chance on another day. However, if you turn it into a shoving match, or give up, this may be their last trip to the edge of forgiveness, especially with you as their tour guide.

STEP 8: REPENT AND TURN TO JESUS

At Perry Park, it was our full intention to continue with the games. But, when the Holy Spirit directed us to stop everything and talk about Jesus, we did so. We made a complete turn of events and went in the opposite direction from what we had planned. That was a complete change of direction, a change of mind, sort of like repentance.

When younger, I thought repentance was the act of apologizing for the wrong things I had done. Well, not exactly. Repentance is a change of mind about Jesus and a complete turning away from the sin you once embraced as your own.

If you are walking down the road of sin you repent when you change your mind and turn the opposite direction down the road toward Jesus. It doesn't mean you will never sin again, but it does mean it's not your purpose to continue sinning. You are now going in another direction and this path takes you straight to the foot of the Cross.

This step of repentance really happens at the same time you make the decision to follow Jesus and accept Him as your Savior. You can't accept him and step toward Him in faith without turning from the direction you were going.

For example, if you constantly lie to your parents, when you accept Jesus you must repent and turn away from lying to your parents. It doesn't mean you will never lie again, but it does mean that is not the plan of your life. You are now walking toward Jesus and lying is something you are doing your best to avoid. If Jesus lives in your heart, when you lie to your parents you will feel bad about it, that's the Holy Spirit convicting you of your sin.

When Indiana Jones stood at the edge of the bottomless pit, he went forward in a direction he would not normally travel. He turned away from the safe direction and instead stepped out over a bottomless pit. At the same time he repented (turned directions), he stepped out in faith. When we repent, we are turning away from sin and stepping toward Jesus at the same time.

STEP 9: COMMIT TO JESUS

"That if you confess with your mouth the Lord Jesus and believe in your heart that God has raised Him from the dead, you will be saved. For with the heart one believes unto righteousness and with the mouth confession is made unto salvation." (Romans 10: 9-10 HCSB)

We commit to Jesus with our believing hearts. By our mouths, we proclaim it publicly. Some like to pray quietly to accept Jesus as their Lord, while others pray aloud for witnesses to hear. By our words, we ask Jesus to come into our heart and become Lord of our life. We are making it public and are not ashamed of what we have done.

This point is where many may get nervous about doing the wrong thing. Let's ease your worry. It is not proper words in the sinner's prayer that saves us; it's the condition of your heart. It is a confession by mouth of what is already going on in our heart. I try to allow the person to form their own prayer if I am leading them to Christ.

The sample prayer I used earlier in this book is good or you can simply tell them how you prayed. Whatever takes place, each person must ask Jesus to save him. Someone else cannot do this part. You cannot be prayed into salvation by Brother Eager Pants. It is a commitment you must make; the prayer is an expression of that choice to commit to Jesus. Here is the sample prayer again for your convenience.

Jesus, I know I am a lost and separated from you. Jesus I can't save myself, so please save me. I am reaching out to you right now and ask you forgive me and come into my heart as Lord of my life. Thank you Jesus for saving me.

STEP 10: YOU WILL BE SAVED

In verses above, I just love those last words: "You will be saved!" Wow, what a reassuring statement. It doesn't say that once we do all this we can submit an application for review or await final word from Saint Peter. It doesn't say we must change our ways then be considered. It's guaranteed, signed, sealed, and delivered: I'm His! All we have to do is be real and true about our need for Jesus and He will save. That's a promise from the ultimate promise keeper.

SO WHAT IS MY PART AGAIN?

Let's wrap this up by making it even easier. Maybe this diagram will do the trick. Look for the part God, you and the lost person plays in the salvation process:

STEPS	GOD	YOU	THE LOST
1. Prayer		x	
2. Drawn by God	x		
3. Witness	x	x	
4. Faith	x		
5. Understanding	x		x
6. Godly Sorrow			x
7. Believe	x		x
8. Repent			x
9. Commit			x
10. Salvation	x		

As you can see in the diagram, you and I have only two parts in the process of salvation. We are to pray and to witness. Prayer is the only part we do alone. When witnessing we are aided by the Holy Spirit. In order to commit these steps to memory you may want to memorize the following short poem. Each step is in order:

I will PRAY and He will DRAW, so you can HEAR the Word of God. God gives FAITH To UNDERSTAND, so you feel SORROW For your sin. If you BELIEVE, REPENT and COMMIT, You will be SAVED you can count on it.

Those who are afraid to tell their friends about Jesus may not understand the part they play in the salvation process. Many believe it is all up to them to make sure someone accepts Jesus as their Savior. That is not true. All we are called to do is pray and tell. Are you ready to do both?

CHAPTER 5. SUCCESS IN WITNESSING

I hope to this point you are convinced that your part is much easier than you once thought. You may be thinking: "If my part is this easy, why do I struggle with witnessing and have to read books like this to learn how?"

The possible answer is because Satan has every reason in the world to convince you it's too hard. He wants your friends and family to die and go to Hell. That is the simple answer. There is a motive behind Satan convincing you this is too hard - a spiritual battle. Satan and his demons do not want you to finish this book. You are a danger because you may lead others to Jesus.

Right now, you are considering becoming a hero to a friend. Satan is going to give you every kind of excuse to prevent you from becoming a witness for Jesus. He would love for you to not finish this book and get back to texting and forget all about witnessing to your friends. Do not let him win. Stay focused on what God is calling you to do. Witnessing to the lost is not something Jesus hopes we will do, it is a direct command.

Let me give you an example. Do you like popcorn? I love popcorn at the movies with extra butter...yummy! I get so much butter it usually soaks through the paper bucket onto my lap. When I was younger it was rare to have popcorn at my house because it was such a chore to make. So a trip to the movies meant popcorn.

Prior to the easy microwave popcorn we have today, I had to work for my popcorn. At my house, there were levels I had to conquer in order to get my popcorn. (I use the word "levels" instead of steps for video game lovers among my readers). Here are the levels I had to win to gain my popcorn prize back in the day:

LEVEL #1: CONVINCE MOM I NEEDED POPCORN

Mom exerted complete control over the stove where the popcorn-making process took place. I was not allowed to turn on the stove due to my restriction from hot surfaces. (So I had a close encounter with burning down our house while drying a GI JOE outfit. Nothing burned ... except the outfit!) But, that was their rule and I had to work around it.

Convincing Mom that I needed popcorn took planning, family involvement and strength in numbers. The process was so long and drawn out it made little sense to cook for only one small person. I had to convince at least one of my sisters, particularly the youngest one, who had all the power, that we both needed popcorn. Once that was done, I had accomplished Level One. It took strength in numbers.

LEVEL TWO: GETTING MOM FROM THE COUCH TO THE KITCHEN

My little sister went to work after I enlisted her. She began by convincing Mom she was on the brink of starvation unless she ate popcorn soon. In came Mom to cook for us. I love it when a plan comes together!

She walked over to the cabinet and pulled out the bag of corn, the oil, the pan and the pan cover. The parts were assembled in the kitchen, and we were ready for Level Three!

LEVEL THREE: HEATING THE STOVE

I would jump up on the counter and scoot as close to the heat source as Mom would allow. (Which wasn't very close.) She would click on the stove; in moments the coils turned red hot. Still alive through Level Three!

LEVEL FOUR: HEATING THE OIL

Mom poured oil into the pan and heated it to the right temperature. I would get squirmy anticipating the next level!

LEVEL FIVE: THE FINAL INGREDIENTS

Once the oil was hot, she poured in the corn and I would lean toward the stove listening for the first pop. It always seemed like forever until I heard the first kernel explode into a fluffy white snack. My only job now was to occasionally peek into the pan to make sure everything was working properly.

Mom would slide the pan back and forth to make sure there was good contact with the hot oil and the kernels. It was so cool watching the popcorn push the top right off the pan! When that happened, it was time to eat. I would hop off the counter, race to my bowl, and wait anxiously to receive my hot popped corn.

Of course, the first serving was poured into my little sister's bowl. I didn't complain since she was my best negotiator. Had she not done her work in Level Two I would have died and never even reached Level three. Game Over. But, the remaining corn was all mine, including those pesky kernels that for some reason forgot to pop and ended up in my bowl. I was always amazed at how many duds were in a bag of popping corn!

Fast forward a few years to see what my daughter must do to eat popcorn. She walks into the kitchen, and opens a microwave mini bag of buttered popcorn, pushes a button on the microwave, waits one minute and 20 seconds, opens it, and eats it. Done. Wow, and she thinks he has it rough.

They have completely removed all the work I just described, and now it's as simple as a push of a button. Now that's my kind of cooking. Imagine all the planning and begging I could have avoided in my younger years had microwave popcorn been invented then. When I failed, I had no one to blame but myself. And I did that well as I pouted and stomped to my room. I am so glad witnessing is not as hard as making popcorn in the 70's!

Luke 19:10, "for the Son of Man has come to seek and to save that which is lost. HCSB."

What was lost? People! Jesus has made it His business to seek and to save them. All I have to say is if Orville Redenbacher can help a 12-year-old cook popcorn, then I have confidence Jesus can help you and I reach the lost. He died for it, so trust Him; He knows exactly what He is doing.

Just agree to be available and willing to be a part of what God is doing around you.

Here is the problem: when it comes to witnessing, many of us are doing it like we cooked popcorn in the 1970's. Long ago, I had to convince someone out of my own power to pop the corn. We look at witnessing as convincing others to get saved. We think that we must be clever in laying out the Gospel so no one could refuse it. And if our efforts fail, then we fail.

When I was not clever enough to reach all the levels for my popcorn, I knew I had failed and blamed myself. I would pout with hurt feelings because I was the one being rejected. Is that how you feel about witnessing? Do you feel rejected when your friend does not accept Jesus? That could mean you are approaching witnessing like cooking popcorn in the 70's.

The problem with that is we think we are being rejected. After a few such tries, we give up altogether. Thinking back to my childhood, had my work for popcorn been met with several "no's" in a row, I would have given up. I would have decided this wasn't for me and started eating raisins instead.

That is what we do with witnessing. We put so much blame on ourselves because we don't understand the full process; consequently, we give up and quit when we hear too many "no's". We then seek other things in our lives to be passionate about that won't make us feel rejected.

Microwave Popcorn

When we look at witnessing in the "microwave popcorn days," we realize we are not in charge of doing all the work. I open the bag and I follow the steps that are left up to me. I can't really go wrong if I input the right time and push "Start". The reason it's so much easier is that someone else has done the hard work.

Understand first that it is not only you who wants to see your friend come to Christ. Jesus paid an enormous price on the Cross to buy your friend's freedom.

The hard work has been done and we now must concentrate on our task of praying and sharing the good news. If we look at it from the standpoint of "microwave popcorn," we realize our work is only a small but important part in the salvation process. Therefore, we are not being rejected when someone does not come to Jesus. If someone doesn't like your microwave popcorn, it's Orville Redenbacher they reject, not you. If someone says no to salvation, it's Jesus they are rejecting ... not you.

Success in Witnessing

Go ahead and ask (I know you are thinking it), "Should I celebrate when I lead someone to Jesus?" Yes you should.

"So what do I do when they say no to Jesus? Get mad and pout?" No, you should not pout because if you witnessed that act of witnessing was your victory. The salvation is God's victory.

So how should we judge our success in witnessing? If we can't take credit for a salvation, and we can't take the blame, then is there success in witnessing at all?

Yes, there is success and we should strive to be very successful in our witnessing. Here is an example of how we win when we witness in God's eyes.

Do you like baseball? Non-sports fans, this won't hurt a bit. You may not like baseball and even if you are not ESPN literate, you will get this. Maybe you saw it take place during a baseball game and it really confused you.

Here is the scenario: A player bunts (hits softly) the ball, is thrown out at first base and then is cheered and given chest bumps in the dugout. If you don't know baseball you may have thought, "Ok, he just got out at first base and his team is giving him high fives? Those boys must really love each other."

Well, not so much. They may love each other but that is not the cause of the chest bumps. Instead they are cheering him for his success. "What success?" Well, what you saw was called a sacrifice bunt. In baseball, it's important to move the runner on base closer to home plate so he has a better chance of scoring. In the right situation, a coach may choose to use the sacrifice bunt. This moves the runner from their current base another step closer to home. Even though the batter may get out in the process, he has succeeded in moving the runner – success!

Let's watch a sacrifice bunt at full speed. A runner is on first base. The coach gives the batter the signal to bunt. He bunts the ball by barely tapping it as it slowly bounces between the pitcher and catcher. The pitcher grabs the ball and throws the batter out at first. The runner is able to move to second base and is now closer to home plate.

The coach is happy, the players in the dugout are happy, the batter is happy and the fans are happy even though the batter is out. Everyone is focused on seeing the big picture of moving the runner to second base, and thus closer to home. When the focus is on the runner, it doesn't matter if the batter gets out or not. Even though the batter would love to move the runner to second without getting out, it wasn't the focus. The focus was on the runner.

Making sense?   If so, welcome to how Jesus views our success in witnessing.

Let's look through God's eyes just a moment and see how we are used in His Kingdom. The home plate is the Cross, where one is saved. We want the lost to come home to the Cross. But in order to do so, they must move from first base all the way around to home plate. The runner is a lost person. How do we advance them closer to home? By witnessing to them.

When we witness, we are successful in moving that person from first to second base even though it may look as though we failed. Even if the door is slammed in our face, we planted a seed. That is success.

Let's look at witnessing in full speed and see what God see's. We bring up Jesus during a conversation with Landon. Landon says he is really not interested. We smile and hand Landon a pocket testament as he walks away. To everyone around it looks like we failed. But we didn't. The focus was on Landon, not on whether we were rejected or not. Because he witnessed Landon moved closer to home. That is success.

The person may reject you and laugh at you; others may see you as a failure. But know this for sure; your reward for your sacrifice awaits you in Heaven. The home team may consider you a failure because you get out. But you are playing for the away team and your audience of One knows what you did for His Kingdom.

How do you succeed in witnessing? Simply by witnessing. The outcome does not change your reward for being obedient. Your reward awaits you whether the person comes to Christ or tells you to go jump in the lake. For you and I, the witness is the victory, not the salvation.

Emma, a youth in the group I taught on Wednesday nights, sent me a text message from the Extreme Conference in Gatlinburg, TN. She accepted Jesus as her Savior! I am so excited and so is she. I was also surprised. During our conversations, in and out of class, she said she was saved. She sat through numerous classes where I shared the Gospel and offered an invitation. Yet, tonight was her night.

Although I would have loved being there to see her accept Jesus, I did get to participate in planting and watering the seeds of salvation along with many others. All those times over the years when Jesus was shared are little sacrifice bunts, little victories. Tonight, I celebrate the victory in Jesus which is salvation.

It's so easy I can't mess up

Before I move away from the popcorn bowl, I would like to make one last point. Ever smelled burnt popcorn? It's terrible and lingers around the house for a long time. If you want to see noses wrinkle, then burn a bag of popcorn during the baseball game. It is so noticeable everyone will know you made a mess of things.

Why do people burn popcorn after Orville Redenbacher went out of his way to make it child proof? Simple: We didn't follow the instructions. We grab the bag and throw it in the microwave guessing at the time to cook. If you don't cook it long enough, you get a sticky mess; if you cook it too long, it really stinks.

It's the same thing with leading someone to Jesus. If you just want to guess your way through the process, you may leave a lot out, overdo it and stink up the room. This is where a little care is required. You must care enough to learn enough about witnessing to others.

CHAPTER 6. BASICS OF WITNESSING

Just over 20 kids sat on the floor of our dark youth room on a Wednesday night. Scriptures written on our walls glowed from the black lights. On this night, all of the kids present had heard the Gospel many times. Most were saved, but not all. They were expecting another class as usual. I walked in and truly felt an overwhelming presence of the Holy Spirit. I could just feel someone was going to be saved that night. Normally my classes will last at least two hours, so the kids had barely settled in when I began speaking.

I can't remember the exact words, but I will summarize. I said, "Jesus came to this earth because you were lost. He died for you; He paid the price for your sin. He was resurrected and He lives right now. If you are lost when you die you will go to Hell. If you are saved you will go to Heaven. Jesus loves you and wants to save you."

I told them I would pray, and when I finished, those who needed to come to know Jesus as their personal Savior should raise their hand. After my prayer, several hands went up and over the next hour some of the mature students and I led four youth to a saving relationship with Jesus Christ.

I'm very long winded so this was my shortest lesson ever! God was in the room; working. That is what caused these youth to suddenly know they were lost and needed Jesus Christ.

You might say, "If that's all it takes, then why does my pastor preach till 12:25 every Sunday afternoon!" Maybe he thinks you need it? Just a thought. This very short lesson worked because God had been at work in these kids' lives for months; tonight was harvest time. Jesus did not need a long sermon. Sometimes He does, sometimes He doesn't. On this particular night, He only wanted an invitation.

Over the course of a few years witnessing and seeing people come to saving faith in Jesus, no two experiences were alike. How can we study a style or pattern of witnessing that works when something may be different every time?

Below I plan to give you the one tool that will never fail you. In studying scripture and from past experience, there is one specific thing that is almost always present.

Techniques and styles and tracts are great and should be used, but if our approach is different every time we witness, we need something more. Do you have this very important tool? Are you prepared to learn one of the most important lessons in witnessing? Good!

MOST IMPORTANT TOOL FOR WITNESSING

Passion.

That was a short answer wasn't it? If you have passion, you will witness. If you have passion, you will learn all you need to know to answer questions about Jesus and tell your story on how you were saved. It will be important to you and you will simply go do it. It won't be a program, it won't be a technique, but it will be a passion, a way of life.

There is one common trait among all the youth and adults I have been around who have witnessed about Jesus. That trait is a passion to see someone saved. That was the most important ingredient determining whether someone would, if the opportunity arose, witness to the lost.

You can know every technique that has been developed to share Jesus, but without passion to see someone saved, your technique will not be put to use. So, my good friend, do you have passion to see others come to Christ?

I will never forget a movie I watched about a missionary traveling overseas to minister to a small settlement. This missionary had led only one man to the Lord since his arrival to this faraway place. One evening, the missionary was having a pity party because he was not being successful at reaching the other people of the village. (Obviously he had forgotten he was playing for the away team and did not see witnessing as the success.)

He was speaking to the only man whom he had led to salvation. The missionary was upset that no one else had come to know the Lord despite his months of work. Then he asked the man, "Why did you believe what I told you about Jesus?"

The man looked at the missionary and said, "I do not think you would come this far just to tell a lie."

I love that part of the movie. It was the missionary's passion that stood out to this lost man. What else causes someone to travel around the globe giving up all the luxuries of America to see someone come to Jesus? A God-breathed passion to do so.

Only passion will cause someone to talk, act, and study in a way that prompts others to come to know Jesus. You will live in a way that others will know something is very different in your life. If you are passionate to see others know the Lord, you will be able to overcome any fear to witness.

John C. Maxwell, in his book, The 21 Indispensable Qualities of a Leader, wrote

"Passion increases willpower – If you want anything badly enough, you can find the willpower to achieve it." If witnessing is a passion, your willpower will allow you to overcome your fear.

John Maxwell also made the point that "passion changes you – In the end your passion will have more influence than your personality." Are you shy? According to John Maxwell, you can influence more people around you than someone with an outgoing personality if you have a passion to do so.

Lastly John Maxwell writes, "Passion makes the impossible possible – Human beings are so made that whenever anything fires their soul, impossibilities vanish. A fire in the heart lifts everything in your life." Your friends will see the fire in your heart when sharing Jesus is a passion. We can try convincing others we love Jesus with our words, but our passion will leave no room for doubt.

YOU CAN'T DO IT JUST ONCE?

Do you recall the Lay's potato chip commercial? It advertised their chips as being so good, "You can't eat just one!" That is so true. I don't think I have ever eaten one chip and just walked away. Normally, I'm stuffing a mouthful of potato chips in my face as I double fist two more handfuls. Witnessing can have the same draw. Once you taste it, you can't get enough.

Witnessing is rewarding and exhilarating. You probably think I've lost my mind. How can something so scary like witnessing be something I can't get enough of? My only explanation is this: it's a God thing. If you don't believe me, prove me wrong. I double dog dare you.

Remember Perry Park? It was there that many of my youth witnessed for the first time. The experience set them on fire to do it again. It is rare to find anyone who has witnessed once that now regrets ever doing so. When a Christian finally gets enough passion to overcome their fear and witness, they want to taste it again.

ALL YOU NEED IS YOUR FIRST TASTE

If you are among the majority who has never witnessed, I invite you to a little experiment. Begin praying today for your first chance to share Jesus.

WARNING: Please be aware, if you begin praying for a chance to witness, it will happen, possibly when you least expect it.

Remember the first time you ever jumped off the diving board at the pool? I do. It took me a long time to be lured out to the end of the board. "Come on, jump off just once!" they yelled. Finally I stepped off the end of the board. Wow!

I loved it! I ran back to the diving board ladder to jump again. That is how witnessing is to a Christian. Once you try it, you want to do it more and more. It seems that you are almost running to the next person so you can tell them about Jesus.

THE NEVER-ENDING SMILE

I was visiting a church and their youth group had the night service to talk about their experience on a recent mission trip. During this mission trip they led 13 people to saving faith in Jesus. Several of the youth witnessed for their first time. These kids simply could not quit smiling. Ever been around youth or adults who have just witnessed for their first time? Here, I will describe what it looks like. Their smile almost touches their ears and it won't go away. It's a never-ending smile.

As each told about their experiences from the trip, the best stories were the ones shared by youth who once thought they could never witness. What a turnaround! They tasted it and wanted more. On the mission field, they would almost race each other to the lost. They did not use any technique the youth minister or pastor taught. It was simply the Holy Spirit overwhelming their heart with love for the lost. It was passion.

Tammy, the Mother of Emily, told my favorite story. Emily, a youth member, had never witnessed and planned to keep it that way as she traveled to the mission destination. However, on the first day, she overcame her fear and witnessed for the first time. After her first taste, she ran back to the group with uncontrollable excitement. She had done it and had acquired the never-ending smile! I have never been able to teach that kind of excitement. It simply must be experienced. Only the power of God can ignite a youth or adult in this way. Emily now wanted to witness to everyone, yet only a week earlier was too fear ridden to do so.

PASSION OVERCOMING FEAR

What happened to Emily is a step we all must take in our lives if we are to witness and teach others to witness. Our passion must overcome our fear. Why could she not witness prior to this mission trip? Because her fear to witness was too strong. It's much easier to avoid our fear than to face the battle.

As she now looks back, Emily will tell you it was worth overcoming her fear to witness. But there was no way of knowing that until she went forward and faced her fear.

WITNESSING WITHOUT THINKING

Tammy continued with her story about Emily. On the way home from the trip, they stopped at a gas station. Tammy felt God moving her to witness to a certain man at the gas station. Up and down the potato chip aisle she paced, trying to build up the nerve to do what God had commanded. Finally, Emily came up and said, "Mom, what are you doing walking in circles?"

"I'm trying to get up enough nerve to talk to those guys about Jesus like God told me to do," Tammy said.

Emily looked at her mom and said, "That's okay Mom, I got it!"

Without missing a beat, Emily grabbed the tract out of her mother's hand and walked right up to those men to witness. That is passion. She tasted it and wanted more. She was witnessing without giving it another thought. No pacing, no hand wringing... she just did it because God had changed her.

Emily would never have done that in her good old hometown just a few days before. She would have run out the door. Now, though, she was running to the lost.

FEAR EATS PASSION FOR LUNCH

My Grandmother, known as Granny by my family and friends, was diagnosed with lymphoma in her lumbar spine in 2007. This type of cancer can be treated aggressively, but at her age it is rare to control or beat. Her physicians suggested a very light dose of chemotherapy.

At age 90, the doctors believed chemotherapy and radiation could cause even more health problems for her. They were not sure if she could handle the treatments necessary to beat this aggressive cancer. It had eaten away bone in her vertebrae at L2 and L3. Not only was overcoming the cancer a huge obstacle, but walking again was doubtful. Her prognosis was poor, to say the least.

Granny has always been independent and a strong Christian, so prayer began immediately with my friends and family. There are many small things that took place due to God answering prayer, such as my sister and brother in law knowing the right doctors. But I want to focus on one specific point: When her passion to live overcame her fear to fight.

Try to put yourself in her shoes. Many in her life had passed on to be with the Lord. She was 90 years old and did not want to become a burden to her family by being unable to care for herself (her words, not mine.) The battle against this cancer would take a lot of money, time, work, travel and sickness. The outcome was unknown.

Most in this situation, at this age, give up. Her initial thought after hearing she had cancer was that she would not get to see her great grandkids grow up. That was her only thought. As they told her the options for survival, each option had its drawbacks.

She could simply give up and go home and enjoy her last days. She could take a light dose of chemotherapy and radiation and slow the cancer's advancement. She could take the full dose of chemotherapy; the option only her family believed was possible. At her age, this was not advisable.

If she survived the fight against cancer, her condition could leave her unable to care for herself. She wanted none of these options. The probable outcome of fighting her cancer could be worse than living out her last days quietly at home.

With these outlooks facing her, it would be understandable to fear the battle and their results more than the cancer itself. Why face all that with an unknown result? What if she went through the treatment and discovers in the end it was not worth fighting? She had to deal with these thoughts.

She chose to fight. Her passion to see her great grandkids grow up was stronger than the fear of the battle or fear of the results. They started her with a light dose of chemotherapy. She tolerated it well. Next they gave her the full dose. Granny was willing to do whatever it took to beat this cancer so she could be with her family a little longer.

THE PATH TO OVERCOME FEAR

I watched Granny take certain steps in her fight to overcome her fear of battling cancer. I think these same steps can be used in our life in witnessing and many others things we are called to do by our Lord.

Diagnosis: Cancer in the lumbar spine.

Your diagnosis: Friends or family who are lost.

Reaction: Prayer. We knew the source of recovery would not come directly from these well-trained physicians. It was from the Great Physician Himself, Jesus Christ, who would bring forth healing through her doctors. Unless it was in God's Will for her to recover, there would be nothing her physicians could do.

Your reaction: Seek Jesus as your source to overcome your fear. If you choose not to cover your fear in prayer you will be doing it all on your own. Prayer is your first step.

Prognosis: Unknown. A good result was not guaranteed. Anything could happen. Inability to walk or care for herself or a prolonged and painful death.

Your prognosis: Unknown. Anything could happen. Rejection, scorn, loss of friends at school or work or being laughed at by your friends.

Her blessing: She knew there was a small amount of hope she could win the battle, enjoy life a little longer and see her great grandkids grow up.

Your blessing: Assured and guaranteed.

"Now the one who plants and the one who waters are equal, and each will receive his own reward according to his own labor." 1st Cor. 3:8 (HCSB)

Jesus made it clear we will be blessed and rewarded when we tell others about Him and disciple others. Blessings will be showered on you here on earth as well as in Heaven. The best news is your reward and blessing will be eternal, amazing and assured.

The edge of decision: It all rested upon what she wanted to do. It was her choice. She stood at the edge of decision. We all wanted her to fight, but we could not force her. It was her battle. Would she go forward into the unknown? If she chose to do nothing, she would never know what the results could have been.

Your edge of decision: It all rests upon what you want to do. It's your choice. Jesus will not force you to be His witness. Although He commanded us to do so, you can refuse. It is unknown here on Earth how many lost souls may not hear the Gospel because you will not tell them. You will never know the results if you turn from the unknown and go take your comfortable seat on your favorite church pew. Not until you stand in Heaven will you see what could have been.

The result: Victory. As I edit this paragraph, Granny is 97 now and I will be picking her up tonight to watch her great granddaughter play basketball. She has seen my son play nearly every baseball and basketball game through his senior year. Her cancer is gone and our prayers answered and she still lives alone. Her blessing is the very thing she desired. Even if this story ended in sad news, the quest to fight would still be my message to you.

Your result: If you choose to overcome your fear, the same steps Granny took can also be your guide. Her footprints are still visible in the sand for us to follow. What will happen is unknown. What is known? People will come to Christ. You may not see every salvation that is a result of your obedience. Your actions may be the sacrifice bunt and you may never know the final result until Heaven reveals it.

What is known? Stepping out on faith to become a living sacrifice for Jesus changes the world around you. Not only will you benefit here on Earth and for eternity in Heaven, but also those around you will benefit.

Life is full of risk. The unknown can be scary sometimes and we can make wrong decisions. Someone with cancer can easily make what appears to be an errant decision. Sometimes fighting may be the wrong decision. Witnessing is not like that at all. Becoming one of Jesus' witnesses will always be the right decision, and this decision will create a ripple effect like that on a calm pond. It will start around you and move outward to others.

Granny's decision stirred every one of us and her ripple has now washed over you. That is how God works. He allows ordinary people to do extraordinary things as a motivator to push others toward greatness.

THE BEST WITNESSING TECHNIQUE, TELL HIS STORY

We all want the best material we can get our hands on to explain the Gospel of Christ. There are many great books that help you develop a technique. There are hundreds of excellent tracts, pocket testaments (www.pocketpower.org) or other handouts to help spread the Word. Find whatever suits your personality. Please keep one thing in mind. You also need to learn how to lead someone to Jesus without any tools, as the chance to witness may occur when you are not carrying a tract or Bible.

No matter where you are, you will discover something new as you witness. If that is the case, how do you prepare?

TIPS TO REMEMBER

Nothing I can write will fully prepare you for what is to come. Jesus will teach you something new every time you witness. But I believe these two simple tips will help you be better at encountering new things on the witness trail.

TIP #1: IF YOU DON'T KNOW, SAY SO

When witnessing to your friend you may find yourself being asked a lot of questions that are tough to answer. Just because you can't answer all these questions doesn't mean you are a weak Christian. There are answers to questions many of us don't know. The mistake is to try answering every question your friend may ask. If you try to answer every question, you will never get to telling them the story of Jesus.

If your friend has a million questions it is ok to tell them you don't know the answer. If you don't know, say so. Then move on to telling them what you do know which is why Jesus came and died for our sins. That is the information they really need before figuring out life's mysteries.

TIP #2: JUST TELL HIS STORY

The best way I have learned to share Jesus is to simply know His Story. Here is what I would suggest. Pick a day when no distractions are expected and get out some paper, your Bible and anything else that tells the story of Jesus. Go through the verses that are important in sharing Christ. Pretend you are writing a summary of a book you just read. If you are good at memorizing scripture add that in as well. Write out in your own words the story of Jesus from beginning to end.

Tip of the week - I believe it is very important that you start at the beginning when sin first entered the world. People need to know the full story. They want to know why Jesus had to die, not only that he did. We must start at the beginning. Let me give you an example.

One day in my children's Sunday School class, I brought in a small book. I opened this book to the middle and read a few pages to them. I then asked they tell me what was happening in this book. They guessed, but they missed the purpose and plot. Why? Because I told the story in the middle of the book. They had no idea what was going on in the book because they didn't know about the beginning. This is exactly what we do most of the time in telling the story of Jesus. If we skip the beginning, we give the impression that Jesus wasn't around until he was born in Bethlehem. We try to only tell the middle of the story when Jesus came to earth.

If you want to know why Jesus died, you will find that in Genesis, in the beginning. If you want to know why we live in a world with death and destruction and why we need a Savior, go to the beginning. I truly believe it will make so much more sense to those to whom you are witnessing when you put the death of Jesus into perspective by telling the complete story.

As you write out your summary, use words you normally speak. Do not use long, difficult words you can't pronounce. Remember, you are recounting a true story. Ban churchy words you have heard and just speak like you do when telling a story of something that happened to you recently. No other story is more powerful or more life changing than that of our Savior.

After writing out how you will tell the story, read it through a few times and keep it in your Bible. Keep it fresh on your mind until you know it by heart.

Below, I have pieced together content this story should include so the recipient will see the full picture of why Jesus came to die for you and me. These topics need to be included in your story. Feel free to add more parts if you want more of the story.

Compile these parts in your story:

- God created everything and it was very good

- No sin, no death

- Adam and Eve created, placed in Garden of Eden

- The Fall, Sin enters the World through Adam

- Separation from God forever due to sin

- The birth of Jesus

- His ministry

- Death on Cross

- We are all sinners, and the cost of sin is death

- All our sins placed upon him and He paid the price

- Dead and buried 3 days

- Resurrection defeated death

- Still lives and is ready to save

- The ABC's of salvation

- How you were saved and what happened

- How it has changed your life (short version)

- Invite them to saving faith in Christ

Add in any scripture if you are good at memory verses.

This may seem like a long list, but once you put it together and learn it as a story, you will remember it. You will be prepared to tell this anywhere at any time, even when caught without your witnessing tracts or Bible.

This is the oldest form of telling others about God, a good true story. There simply is no special secret to leading others to Christ. It really is easier than what you may think. The hard part is deciding you will do it.

If you need a sample prayer the one below can be added at the end of your story.

SAMPLE PRAYER

Jesus, I know I am a lost sinner drowning in this world separated from you. Jesus I can't save myself, so please save me. I am reaching out to you right now and ask you forgive me and come into my heart as Lord of my life. Thank you Jesus for saving me.

Once you have witnessed and the person wants to come to Jesus, the steps outlined in Chapter 2 will help. It is great to use a pocket testament or tract if you have one available.

MY ACTIONS = MY WITNESS

There is a form of witnessing we don't like to talk or think about. Yet we do it daily - our actions.

Jacob and Ben are hanging out between classes playing with their new cell phones. Two weeks ago Jacob had given a pocket testament to Cody and asked him if he knew Jesus. Cody really didn't want to talk about it but he took the testament to read later. Cody had been reading the testament. As Cody walked by Jacob and Ben a few days later he overheard the curse words in the song coming from their cell phone. Cody wasn't shocked by the song, but he was surprised at who was playing it.

What did Jacob and Ben do at this moment? They ruined their witness. Though Jacob didn't realize it, Cody had been watching Jacob. Jacob claimed to be a Christian and different. "Was he though", Cody wondered. When Cody was going to bed that night he noticed the pocket testament on his dresser. He tossed it in the trash and went to bed.

Why did this happen? Why did Cody go from reading the pocket testament to tossing it the trash? Because the one who cared enough to give him the pocket testament turned out to be just like everyone else. We call this being a hypocrite. Saying you're a Christian one day but not acting like it. Here is a tip that will help you witness. If you decide to be a witness for Jesus it is much more than handing out tracts and talking about Jesus. It's about acting like you are different even when you think no one is looking.

Will you and I be able to act perfect all the time? Nope, won't happen. But we must be aware that those we are witnessing to are watching everything we do. If you want your friend to know Jesus can make him different, he must first see the difference in you.

Your friends will respond to hearing about Jesus more when they can easily tell you are different. Quit trying to be like everyone else and be who Jesus made you to be. We won't convince our friends Jesus changes lives by our words, but by our actions.

THE DIVINE APPOINTMENT

One of the toughest things to do for most Christians after they know how to tell the story is to receive the opportunity to do so. Many of us are simply not skilled at moving a conversation from the ball game to Jesus. So what is the best way to have the opportunity to witness?

I believe the best way to share Christ is by showing up to a Divine Appointment.

A Divine Appointment is a moment in time when you and another person come together on what seems to be a chance meeting. However, Jesus has His amazing nail scarred hands all over it.

When I have an appointment, there are at least two people who know. I will know and the one I am meeting will know. That's the way I set up a meeting. As long as we both know the date, time, place and purpose of the meeting, we are good to go.

A Divine Appointment, however, is just the opposite. God will not send you a text message in advance to find a "good time" for you. He doesn't check your calendar to make sure you are interested in witnessing at 1:30 p.m., this Thursday. You will not know when the Divine Appointment is going to take place. All you will know ahead of time is that you have asked God to set up a meeting. The rest is up to Him.

This is my favorite way to witness, as I completely leave it up to God. Since God is already at work, why not allow Him to set up the appointments with those whom He is working. God will know the lost souls who need to hear the Gospel.

WHY USE DIVINE APPOINTMENTS?

There are many ways to witness. Some choose to knock on doors and hand out flyers or tracts as they walk down a city street. While on mission trips, we witness to those who respond to a performance or event we set up. We witness to our friends during conversations. These all are ways to experience a Divine Appointment. There are so many different ways and avenues open to witness. I believe the Divine Appointment is also a great way to bring the story of Christ to the lost. Here are some reasons why.

REASON #1 ALWAYS A PURPOSE

I had an appointment to meet with a student who was lost. He knew he was lost and was very happy remaining that way. His cousin, sister and mother wanted me to come speak with him about salvation and also debate creation versus evolution, a favorite topic of mine. So we set up an appointment to meet with him one day after school.

We all met in their living room and started talking about creation versus evolution. It wasn't quite the debate we thought it would be. He really had no defense of evolution, since there isn't one. Then I began to share Jesus. As we neared the end, I felt like this was not worth the time we spent. He clearly didn't care what I had to say about creation or Jesus.

But...there was a purpose to this meeting. His mother began asking questions and it became clear the Holy Spirit was convicting her. It was as if the Spirit had to jump up and down to show me I wasn't there for the son; I was there for the Mother. After another hour of discussion, she accepted Christ as her Savior.

There is always a purpose to a Divine Appointment. I thought I knew the full purpose of going to this home. I knew the time, date, place and the person I was meeting. But I was wrong about the purpose. But the One Who set up the appointment, Jesus, knew what needed to be accomplished. So always leave the purpose up to the Jesus.

REASON #2: THE APPOINTMENT MAKER IS ALWAYS RIGHT

In John Chapter 17, Jesus is told his friend Lazarus is very sick and close to death. Jesus didn't exactly rush to get there. By the time Jesus arrived Lazarus had been dead for four days! Many might say he missed his appointment to save his friend from death. But, once again, the Appointment Maker was exactly right on time. It was done to Glorify God. To this day that event is taught in our churches as an inspiring truth of how God is always on time even when we think he is late.

Just think about it this way. In the "ten steps of salvation," we see God at work drawing the lost to Him so we can share His story. Doesn't it make sense that God will also set up the time for him or her to hear? I think that is very clear. I want to be sharing the Gospel with those God is actively drawing to Him.

REASON #3: HIS APPOINTMENTS ARE BETTER THAN MINE

Here is the diagram from earlier in the book. Notice again the work around us by God. God draws the person, the Holy Spirit works with you as you witness, and He convicts the Lost of their sin while giving faith and understanding and the ability to believe. Look over the diagram again.

STEPS	GOD	YOU	THE LOST
1. Prayer		x	
2. Drawn by God	x		
3. Witness	x	x	
4. Faith	x		
5. Understanding	x		x
6. Godly Sorrow			x
7. Believe	x		x
8. Repent			x
9. Commit			x
10. Salvation	x		

With all this work going on by God, why would we try to take matters into our own hands and witness where God is not working? I want to be right in the middle of where God is doing His work so that my efforts can Glorify Him.

108

My purpose of witnessing is not to make myself feel better because I did something for God. Nor is it to do a work or impress someone. It is to see others come to Christ or at least plant a seed where God wants it planted.

If I am working on my own, I am missing out on playing for the away team. I will not be sacrifice bunting someone closer to home with Jesus. I am simply running around making myself feel good that I have done something for Jesus.

But if I seek The Holy Spirit to lead me into a Divine Appointment and keep myself open to His guidance, I will be in the right place, at the right time, and speaking to the right person.

DIVINE APPOINTMENT REQUIREMENTS

1) Pray God sets up a Divine Appointment so you can witness.

2) Be watchful for the appointment.

3) Respond to the appointment.

DIVINE APPOINTMENTS AT SCHOOL OR WORK

So how do Divine Appointments work in school or work? Here is a great example. Suppose Sam has a friend, Jed, who does not know Jesus. Sam wants the opportunity to share his faith with Jed. He really wants Jed to at least be prepared to listen.

Sam begins by praying for Jed. Then Sam asks God to set up a Divine Appointment with Jed and prepare Jed's heart. The reason Sam does this is because without God working in someone's life they will not be saved. So instead of Sam guessing at the right time to share Jesus, he prays Jesus will set up the appointment. Sam will need to be prepared and ready and watching for an opportunity to talk with Jed about Jesus.

How will Sam know it's the right time? Sometimes you just know. It may be from Jed saying something that opens up the conversation or something may happen that allows Sam to bring up Jesus. The appointments are usually noticeable but they are also easy to walk away from.

Be ready for the chance to share Jesus at any moment. You will know when it's time to talk about Jesus as the Holy Spirit will let you know in some way. Here are some other types of appointments which may happen outside school or work.

TYPE 1: GOD POINTS OUT THE DIVINE APPOINTMENT

Clair Nelson, a former youth member, is able to see through God's eyes in amazing ways. It happens often for her simply because she prays God will allow her to see through His eyes. Remember, God answers prayers.

Often The Holy Spirit will lead her to speak with someone who was too shy to speak to her. It's not always the Christian who is nervous to talk about Jesus; the lost are sometimes as well. Clair has had the opportunity to witness to countless people simply because she asked in prayer to see through God's eyes. Amazing what we are given if we will only ask.

I wish I could say God will provide a huge arrow pointing at the person, but it is much more subtle than that. It is sometimes a feeling that you need to talk to a certain person. Many of you right now are probably saying to yourself, "Hey, I have felt that before! I felt the pull to go speak to a certain person about Jesus." What happens most of the time is that we question it, think about it and hesitate until the Divine Appointment has passed.

That is why so many of us miss our meeting God sets up. I have missed numerous appointments because I was in a hurry or doubted. I realize it later after my chance has passed and it is heartbreaking. On top of it all I then recall I had prayed for a Divine Appointment. God did His part, yet I failed to show up.

I recall a Divine Appointment Clair had during our youth performance in Clarksville, Tennessee. After a performance at a church, I led an invitation; several teenagers came forward to pray. Clair felt The Holy Spirit tug at her heart to speak to one particular girl. Though several were at the altar, she was drawn to this one girl. Clair asked if she wanted to talk. She shook her head no and looked away.

I would have walked away at that point, thinking I misread The Spirit's leading. Clair trusted that The Holy Spirit had told her to speak to this specific girl, so after a few minutes Clair asked again. This time the girl wanted to talk. After a long conversation she accepted Jesus as her personal Savior.

Later we found out a Deacon in the Church had been working with the girl for years and many were praying she would come to Christ. This Deacon had passed away a few months earlier. The seeds had been planted and watered for years. Clair simply followed God's lead and looked through His eyes to be that final sacrifice bunt to bring her home to Christ.

When you pray for a Divine Appointment, you should be ready immediately. From the moment you lift up your eyes, you must begin expecting someone to come into your path. You must be looking with anticipation and wondering whom it will be that you are to witness to. The moment you get the feeling to talk with someone, do it. Do not hesitate or second guess yourself. That will only lead to missing out on an amazing appointment God has set up especially for you.

When Clair prays to see through God's eyes, she immediately opens her eyes expecting to see whatever God wants to show her. There is no doubt in her heart whether God will work; she fully expects and believes He will. And in His time, He does.

Many Divine Appointments will take place in church or religious event settings. But on occasion our appointments will arrive completely unannounced out of the blue.

TYPE 2: MY APPOINTMENT JUST SHOWED UP

Another way God sends appointments our way is by chance meetings. Brandy Nelson, a former youth member, told me a story that had happened to her. As I wrote this book, Brandy was serving as a mission intern at Houston First Baptist Church in Texas. During a break, she and another intern were sitting on the front porch of a nearby apartment as a rainstorm passed through Houston. They were enjoying the coolness of the rain, a nice break from the Texas heat. That is when the appointment just showed up.

A man walked past, completely drenched from the downpour. Brandy asked if he wanted to step up on their porch and out of the rain. He did, and they struck up a conversation. He had "accidentally" walked one street too far and missed where he was supposed to go. Isn't that so often how it works? That was such an odd thing to happen, but if he had not missed his road, he would have missed his appointment with Brandy.

Their conversation eventually came to the subject of Jesus. Brandy didn't force the subject. The Holy Spirit slowly guided the conversation like a hand on the steering wheel. There was so much that confused the man, so Brandy explained things about Jesus and His forgiveness. The storm kept this man on the porch while the Holy Spirit worked in his heart. After a long discussion, this man accepted Christ as his personal Savior.

Was this totally random and unexpected? To Brandy and the man it was. But to God this was a Divine Appointment. Booked and scheduled before the world was even formed. Brandy did not know the date, time, place or purpose but she agreed to show up by praying for a Divine Appointment and a man's eternal life changed.

Look at all the "ifs" in this story. What if he would not have missed his road while walking? Hey, I have missed a lot of roads in my life when driving, but this guy was walking! It's hard to miss a road while walking, unless perhaps God sent an angel to help lure him just a little farther down the road.

What if it had not been raining? There would be no reason to come up on the porch. What if Brandy had not asked him to come out of the rain? What if Brandy was not in Houston as an intern? What if this man had refused to come up out of the rain? What if God was not working in his heart? Do you see how everything had to come together to work?

This seemed so random and coincidental. Yet, there was no doubt this was arranged by the most amazing appointment maker in the Universe! It was all meant to happen and Brandy agreed to do her part at this Divine Appointment. In his quest to find shelter from the rain he found eternal security in the arms of Jesus.

The most important thing to remember about Divine Appointments is be prepared, ready and watching. We never know when the next appointment will show up or when God may point out your next appointment. It will usually happen when you least expect it. Start praying now that God will set up a Divine Appointment with someone you know or a stranger and start watching for it.

Do Divine Appointments always work?

Sometimes, your Divine appointment will be rejection. Does this mean you misread your feeling or didn't really see through God's eyes? Not at all. If you felt the need to speak to someone in Christ's name, then there was a purpose. I would suggest there are three common situations that may

happen during a Divine Appointment beyond someone
accepting Christ:

1. No Deal

There is a time of anticipation when witnessing to a lost
person. We want our friend to get saved as soon as possible.
But what about when they don't come to Jesus?

Many times I am saddened to see someone walk away from
the invitation to know Jesus. I could only respect that
decision and let them know the invitation is always open.
Those times are disappointing. Did that mean it was not a
Divine Appointment? Of course not! Remember the analogy
of the sacrifice bunt. These "sacrifices" are necessary to
advance that person closer to Jesus, and you were either
sowing a seed or watering the seed. Either way, when you
share the Gospel with someone and the door is slammed in
your face, you have done your part at the appointment.

Jenna was recently playing at a birthday party and asked a
girl while playing if she knew Jesus. The girl replied she
"didn't want to talk about Him and did not want to know
about getting saved." Was this not a Divine Appointment?
Yes it was. Jenna felt like she should say something and she
did. Jenna was successful because she witnessed and planted
a seed. She made a sacrifice bunt for the away team.

2. Already Saved

Another situation is when the person already knows Jesus.
It's easy to walk away from that moment thinking we did not

see through God's eyes. Instead of seeing a lost person, we saw a saved person. Is this reason to doubt our ability to see through God's eyes or recognize a Divine Appointment? Not at all.

Whether you will know here on Earth or not, it had a purpose. Maybe the purpose was to influence the other Christian to do likewise. Almost every time this happened, the other Christian had a positive reaction that someone was out witnessing. It encouraged that saved person to do the same thing.

During a summer mission, Clair attended a Divine Appointment with a lady at a Laundromat. After asking the lady about her relationship with Jesus, Clair learned the woman was already saved. She invited Clair and the rest of us to come to her store the next day so she could give Clair a special gift. This lady owned a shirt store and Clair was given a shirt of her choice. This lady wanted to bless Clair for her boldness to witness. I see that as a way God blessed her for showing up at the Divine Appointment.

3. YOU ARE A "NO SHOW"

A very good friend of mine, Josh Patton, was on a mission trip to Charleston, South Carolina, the summer before his freshman year in college. He had already surrendered to the ministry. He experienced a "See through God's Eyes" Divine Appointment. This is his story in his own words.

"One day during our free time, we went to the beach. I was not very impressed with this beach and didn't really want to get in the water. Instead I walked up and down the beach. I was thinking about the week and God and what he wanted in my life. I thought about how shy I was when it came to one on one sharing of my faith. I would lead a Bible study or preach anytime I was asked but it made me very uncomfortable to just strike up a conversation with a person about God. As I was thinking about that, God convicted me. He showed me a woman he wanted me to share my faith. I argued and decided it wasn't really God telling me to witness, only my own thoughts."

"So I presented God with a test, not sure what I was thinking there. The woman was walking her dog on a leash. I told God that if He really wanted me to talk to that woman then let the dog run out in front of me. This is not a hard story to figure out; of course the dog ran out in front of me and forced an interaction with the woman. Then at that moment of truth I smiled and continued walking. As I walked away, I thought about how I should go back and talk to her, but I never got the courage."

"That woman could be the strongest Christian that ever walked the face of the earth or she could have been lost and have never heard about Jesus. I will never know because I was too afraid to witness to her. I think about that story every time I hear someone talk about fear in witnessing."

Josh was a no show at this Divine Appointment. God set up a time for Josh to witness but he didn't.

Do you trust God is at work around you? We must be challenged to have childlike faith that God is working around us all the time. We must be on constant lookout for an appointment.

It's time to test your faith that God is working around you and is prepared to use you. At the end of this chapter, pray that God will send you a Divine Appointment. Once you pray be alert. The appointment may just happen at any time, or it may be a week later. It may happen while eating in the lunchroom or at the ballgame. It may happen to be with someone totally unexpected or a friend you have known for years. God will be faithful in setting up an appointment. Will you be faithful and show up?

God will work and send you a Divine Appointment sometimes sooner than you expect. Will you be ready? If you want to use a tract or pocket testament order them now. Get your story of Jesus together now. If you do not begin you will not be ready when the Divine Appointment takes place and you will be a "no show."

Witnessing should be done your way. God created us all different. You may be able to walk up and tell the story of Jesus easily to anyone who will listen or you may be shy. No matter your personality you can witness. You may love using a bracelet with different colors to explain the Gospel. You may like telling His story or handing out tracts. You may need a tool to help show others how to come to Jesus. Find what works for you and just do it.

CHAPTER 7. THE NEXT GENERATION

When I was younger, I heard people say how terrible things were getting in America. Some things never change. I still hear that. I could make a list longer than this book verifying how bad things are out there with our young people. Our God is being tossed aside by a nation that has forgotten. America has forgotten to whom the founding mothers and fathers bowed their knees. We forget that this is the greatest nation on Earth because of God, not in spite of Him.

I could continue ranting, but I would rather spend my time focusing on the positive. I have found that many of our youngest Christians, like you, are absolutely hungry for something real. You want to be held accountable. You want to be challenged in your spiritual walk. You want to be part of something larger than yourself. You want to be part of changing the world around you by sharing your faith in Jesus. If you do that, you can change things. It starts with you.

Jesus is real. He's mysterious and wild and exciting. He's everlasting. Here is something very important for you to remember. America has taken down the Ten Commandments from our school walls. Many citizens and government officials have figured out a way to stop public prayer in our school classrooms. They have banned the Gideon's and their Bibles. But so far, they have not discovered a plan to keep a sixth grader from sharing Jesus with her friend.

Unleash the power of the Holy Spirit in your school through sharing Jesus and things will change.

You are being called out to the battlefield. It is time to lead others to Jesus. Someone, somewhere, now, waits on you to be a hero to One.

WHAT NOW?

This is your call to action. We are in this together. We can learn from others in our witnessing efforts. When I read another's story of how they witnessed to a friend I become encouraged. When I read a story about someone who never gave up on their friend, it gives me a boost to continue. This is why I created a website specifically for witnessing stories. Each time you witness, no matter the outcome, it becomes a learning experience. That experience should be shared with others. On this website it can be.

I invite you now to join us on our website at www.iwillwitness.com. I plan to read everyone's experience and you can also ask me questions personally from my website. I hope to hear from you! What an opportunity to be part of an online community of everyday Christians sharing Jesus.

Whether you have been rejected, handed out a tract or led your friend to saving faith your story has a place on our website. Not only will your story encourage others but you may be encouraged by what you read. I look forward to hearing from you. Add your story today to the website, it may change the heart of another forever.

NOW, LET'S SEE WHAT GOD DOES NEXT!

Dictionary

Upon hearing a long churchy word I want to raise my hand, stop the pastor in his tracks and ask for a definition. But when he's on a roll who can interrupt? In this book you will run across some of those words. No need to worry, I am providing a churchy word dictionary for you.

Age of Accountability : When a young person first understands the gospel of Jesus, our sin and our need to be saved.

Audience of One : God is always watching us and all we do. God is our constant audience.

Conviction: The Holy Spirit makes us aware that we are sinners and our need for Jesus to forgive us.

Gospel: The "good news" about Jesus - His life, death and Resurrection to save you from sin.

Hero to One: When you share your faith with someone you become a hero to that person whether you realize it or not.

Holy Spirit : The Third Person of the Trinity through whom God acts. The Holy Spirit helps us to witness and is active in convicting the hearts of the lost. We can't see the Holy Spirit but we can see His work around us.

Lost: Someone who does not have a personal relationship with Jesus.

Rewards in Heaven: In Heaven there will be a time when Jesus gives rewards to those who did things on earth in His Name. Although we don't deserve these rewards He will give them.

Resurrection: God raised Jesus to life from death after 3 days.

Salvation : A rescue from sin and death that takes place the moment you ask Jesus into your heart.

Sanctification : God separates you from the world and from Satan to become His as He grows you more like Christ. It is a major part of the Salvation process as we are set apart to God.

Saved : Those who have accepted Jesus as their personal Savior and will one day enter Heaven after death here on earth.

Sin : Anything we do that rebels against God and causes us not to live out our Godly purpose on earth.

Spiritual World : The part of the world we can't see with our eyes where Angels, Demons, Satan and God work and exist. We can't see them at work but we can see their effects.

The World: Things all around us that are sinful and pull us away from Jesus.

Witness: To share the story of Jesus Christ with others in many different ways including our actions.

ABOUT THE AUTHOR

Wade White lives in Lyon County, Kentucky and is a father of two, Brandon and Jenna. Married to Dee Dee for 25 years. He is a graduate of the University of Kentucky with a major in Political Science and minor in History. Wade has been a youth minister for over 14 years and currently attends Southside Baptist Church in Princeton, KY. Wade was elected as the Lyon County Judge Executive in 2011, and is currently serving his second term.

Wade is the founder of Revive Prayer Walk which spread across many locations in America giving rise to prayer walking at local schools. Wade plans to be releasing his next book soon about these prayer walks and how others across America can put together a monthly prayer walk for your local school.

In conjunction with this book Wade created a webpage that allows readers to tell their own witnessing stories. It may be a story of how you fear witnessing, how you overcame the fear, or other stories of witnessing. Wade believes we can learn from each other's experiences and he looks forward to personally reading your story on the website. Feel free to visit the website with your story of witnessing at www.iwillwitness.com.

ONE LAST THING...

If you enjoyed this book or found it useful I'd be very grateful if you'd post a short review on Amazon. Your support really does make a difference and I read all the reviews personally so I can get your feedback and make this book even better.

If you'd like to leave a review then all you need to do is visit this books page on Amazon and leave your review.

Thanks again for your support! Now go play for the away team!

Wade White

REFERENCES

John C. Maxwell, The 21 Indispensable Qualities of a Leader

(ttp://www.fallenbrothers.com/community/showthread.p hp?t=1708

Coming Down From the Hero High

Bob Yehling   Page 139   4/25/2009Copyright 2002
Newhouse News Service

All Rights Reserved

Newhouse News Service...03/20/2002

By Mike Celizic

TODAYShow.com contributor

updated 8:31 a.m. CT, Mon., June. 11, 2007

Made in the USA
Monee, IL
26 January 2023

26281139R00080